✕

To Dan & Lula for loving
and caring for me when
it mattered most...

good food
to come
home to

www.mascotbooks.com

Farm Girl In The City: Of Food and Love

©2018 Bonnie McDaniel. All Rights Reserved. No part of this publication may be reproduced, stored in a retrieval system or transmitted in any form by any means electronic, mechanical, or photocopying, recording or otherwise without the permission of the author.

For more information, please contact:
Mascot Books
620 Herndon Parkway #320
Herndon, VA 20170
info@mascotbooks.com

LCCN: 2017913657

CPSIA Code: PRTWP0218A
ISBN-13: 978-1-68401-579-5

Printed in Malaysia

Farm Girl In The City

Of Food and Love

Bonnie McDaniel

Contents

For Mac...

This book is dedicated to the one person who has always supported me, even when he did not understand what I was doing. He has dried my tears, held my hand to lift and steady me during those times when life knocked me down. He is a wonderful provider, confidant, and my best friend.

Mac, I never knew when we met so long ago that my life would be as rich and as full of adventure as it has been, and the best part is, you have been right there beside me every step of the way.

For forgiving me for my many faults and applauding my successes, thank you. And, for being my personal food critic and taster of all my new creations, thank you. Thank you too for your patience with me each time I promised not to dig another hole in the lawn and then did just the opposite because I found a tree or a flower that I simply could not resist.

You know me better than anyone I know; my good parts and my flaws, and still you love me. And for taking the time to listen to me go on and on about a discovery I made while cooking or working in the garden, even though I know you were humoring me on most occasions, thanks.

For loving and supporting our two beautiful, crazy kids and for the patience and grace you have extended them through their many ups and downs, thank you. We have seen them go through so many changes and challenges and at times I did not think I would make it through. And just when I thought I could take no more, you reminded me that we had poured our very best into them and that in the end, everything that we had given, like good cream, would rise to the top.

This book has been a dream of mine for so many years and for keeping me honest and not allowing me to make excuses as to why it should not get done, thank you. For your patience with photographers and camera crews traipsing through our home at all hours when most people are still sleeping, thank you.

I only pray that there were just a few moments of joy for you as you waited patiently for me to be where God has determined I should be.

"Love is patient, love is kind, it does not boast and is long suffering." Mac I can truly say that in you I have found the ultimate manifestation of God's love.

Dreams really do come true. Thank you for loving and caring for me and our beautiful family and for making my dream a reality.

XOXO!

Foreword

This is much more than a cookbook. This is a reflection on what makes a strong foundation. It will help you appreciate your family legacy and communicate it authentically.

When you first meet Bonnie McDaniel, you are struck by her deep sense of self. It is easy to be enraptured by her confidence and beauty, but just beyond her external strength is a woman grounded in faith and love for family – an ability to nurture and be nurtured back. Bonnie has a keen eye for knowing what drives people and gravitates towards those in need. She is built from love and expresses love to those around her.

Of Food and Love is Bonnie's story, but it is also your story, or at least a story we need to be telling more often. Today our world can feel as if it is full of difficulty, loss, and disunity. We need to be ever diligent to tell stories of goodness in life, to share our love and support for others in ways that are deeply meaningful and transformative.

Throughout Bonnie's career and life, she has built a Good Living brand – a lifestyle that reflects itself in the bounty of well-cultivated gardens, delicious presentations of food, and a simple approach to living. And while these are the "harvests" of her life's work, in a deeper way she is conveying a focus that is centered on ritual, sharing, and nurturing love with those whom you come into contact.

"the *harvests* of her *life's work*"

Bonnie and I both share a deep love for our grandmothers – Lula and Lucie. They both grew up farm-girls, one from Georgia, the other from California. The generational legacies our grandmothers leave each of us is powerful. We wouldn't be who we are without them, their confidence, their love, and their loyalty. They grew up in different times – some things easier, and others much more difficult – and through their tribulations and triumphs, they shared a deep love for their granddaughters. They guided us. Their teachings are foundational to who we are and we are passing a piece of their insight to the next generation. Lula provided Bonnie with a strong spiritual foundation, taught her the value of serving others, to cherish family and the importance of sharing Sunday Supper with family and close friends. Lucie taught me to value life-long learning and a deep commitment to family. Each employs ritual and manifests itself by conveying love for others and, maybe more importantly, ourselves.

Of Food and Love will give to you and it will nudge you. It will share beautiful recipes and approaches to a simpler life and challenge you to share more of yourself with others. Oftentimes society teaches us that when we give, we lose - but the reality is just the opposite. When we share ourselves with others, through story, through conversation, through good food, we communicate deeply with those around us. Sharing with others is the heart of a nurturing love.

Enjoy this "well beyond" cookbook. Live, learn, share, and enjoy. As Bonnie says, it will help you to "be well and thrive" today and tomorrow.

—**Jessica N. Grounds**,
Women's leadership advocate and
founder of Mine the Gap

This is my life!
A Farm Girl, living in the city!

I grew up in a small country town in Central Florida, in a very close-knit neighborhood called Tucker Hill. You know, the kind of neighborhood where everyone claimed everyone as a relative - even if you were not blood-related. And although it has been decades since I left Tucker Hill, my love for living simply and maintaining a sense of family and community has been ever-present; no matter where I have lived.

When my husband and I purchased our *farm in the city* homestead nearly two decades ago, it was always with the intent of creating a haven for our family and friends with all the elements of simple, country living; in the midst of the hurried lives being played out all around us. Having an abundance of fresh vegetables and herbs for my home-cooked meals and beds of beautiful flower gardens surrounding my home, has through the years, been an integral part of who I am.

A gem of a house with good bones and expansive grounds on which to plant flowers and grow all the foods we love to eat, this special place has been the inspiration for all that I have been able to create and share as a part of my Good Living brand for nearly two decades.

For me, every good recipe begins with inspiration and is built on a good foundation!

And for my kitchen, the inspiration and foundation are grounded in the basics which includes fresh ingredients from the garden, a well-stocked cupboard, go-to's in the fridge, goodness-extenders in the freezer, and, last, but not least, a few good staple kitchen and garden tools to make it all come to together.

Of Food and Love takes the mystery out of cooking some of the staples that I grew up with and also shares the important role food plays in our physical and emotional well-being. It is meant to inspire every new cook or seasoned cook to make your kitchen the center of all that is good in your home. Whether an experienced cook who is seeking inspiration, or the novice who does not know where to begin, Of Food and Love will gently guide you to fall in love with good and inspire you to create that goodness for those you love.

I was raised by who I think was the most incredible cook ever to grace this planet, my grandmother, Lula Duncan. Born and raised in Georgia, this very petite woman, was for me, the epitome of what a good homemaker should be. She married my grandfather, who was in those days, a sharecropper in Georgia, who would later move his family to Ocala, Florida, where he would buy his own farm; raise sugar cane, vegetables and livestock; which included chickens, goats, cows and pigs and use it to raise a family of six children.

At our home, in town, my grandmother kept a very large kitchen garden in addition to fruit and nut trees and from this she formed the foundation for the amazing recipes that graced our kitchen table. She was for me the ultimate example of how to create good food through love, hence the inspiration behind this, my first cookbook.

By the time I came along my grandparents had built a homestead in a section of town called Tucker Hill, which to me will always be my home. Many of my family members continue to reside there on the property purchased by my grandparents and over the years it has been a place where I go to reignite the inspiration that was instilled in me so many years ago. It was my beginning and has served as the foundation of what

has motivated me over the years to create for my family the gifts that I pray will last them over the course of their lifetimes.

It was on Tucker Hill that I developed a love for the garden and where the secrets of "birthing" good food was born. And although I have traveled to some of the most fascinating and intriguing places on the planet and eaten at some of the best restaurants in the world, my basic understanding of love and good food always takes me back to my Tucker Hill home.

Part of my journey has included realizing a childhood dream to share what I experienced growing up, by opening and operating a restaurant, bakery, and boutique hotel/inn. Using my basic foundation, I was able to build a business that resulted in me winning numerous coveted food awards, one of which included my most treasured, the prestigious Wine Spectator award. This award was presented to my restaurant with the distinction of having one of the best food and wine menus in the world. What was most eye-opening for me having won this award was the fact that my restaurant was in competition with restaurants run by chefs who were trained in some of the most acclaimed culinary schools around the world, and yet, it was my basic approach to using fresh and good ingredients that made this achievement possible.

Of Food and Love has been decades in the making, and finally its time has come. It is my desire to not only share good recipes, but also to impart the spirit of what it means to nurture through food. It is also my hope that Of Food and Love will inspire you to create your own sense of good and share that goodness with those you love.

From my Tucker Hill beginnings of home to yours…

—Bonnie,
Farm Girl In The City

"To everything there is a season, a time for every purpose under the sun —
a time to plant and a time to gather that which has been planted."

THE
BASICS

✳

So often I am asked by friends what is the "secret sauce" for my recipes and my answer is always the same; good ingredients and lots of love. What is important to note about this statement is that although I spend a lot of time cooking, these elements do not necessarily equate to you having to spend hours and hours in the kitchen; it is in fact something that is achievable by anyone who is willing to invest the time to learn a few important basics.

Springtime begins the cycle for our kitchen garden as perennial herbs begin to peek through the rich soil. These basic herbs, vegetables and vine fruit are a good way to build the foundation to create most traditional favorites.

Over the years, I have had many people share with me that they are not quite sure how to use the right blend of herbs for their recipes. What is interesting and what a lot of people miss is that your sense of smell when coupled with taste is an excellent way to know what to use. Don't be afraid to experiment. I cannot tell you how many hot messes I have made in the kitchen when trying out something new. But, I did not allow it to stop me from trying until I got it right.

Keep in mind too that if you are short on time or lack the space to grow your own vegetables and herbs, this list of basics can also serve as a guide of what to look for when visiting your local market. These are the basics and from here only your imagination is the limit.

✳

HERBS

Basil This herb is the star in Italian cooking and shows up quite often in Thai cuisine. There are a variety of basils on the market so don't be shy about exploring. In your exploration, be sure to check out the Thai variety which has a very different and stronger flavor and more pungent aroma than the more common sweet Mediterranean basil. A great addition to recipes such as tomato sauces, eggplant dishes and it is absolutely exquisite in pesto.

Cilantro Also known as coriander, this herb is very similar in appearance to flat-leafed parsley but with a distinctively different flavor. This is a must-ingredient for kebabs, curry and salsa. And if you grow it in your own garden or if you are lucky enough to purchase with the roots intact, you are in for a treat as the flavor of the roots is very intense and wonderful in curry pastes.

Dill A native plant from Southern Europe and Western Asia, this herb is a standard in gardens from Spain to Italy. As a matter of fact, it is not uncommon to find it growing wild in these regions. My absolute favorite in potato and egg salad and a great addition to fresh cucumber and zucchini. I also use it to create a savory butter sauce with an addition of lemon and olive oil for the best grilled salmon ever.

Thyme A native of the Mediterranean, thyme has a wonderful aroma and is a favorite herb for most cooks. Like basil, thyme can be found in a number of varieties; lemon being one of the most popular. A must for slow-cooked dishes, it is also a nice companion to tomatoes, zucchini, eggplant and bell peppers. Great in marinades for beef, lamb, pork and game, it is also an essential in stuffing, pates, and terrines. For an unusual treat, add a bit to scrambled eggs or to lentil soup.

Rosemary A very strong herb, rosemary has an intense flavor and is usually used only in meat dishes because of its intensity. Use it to wake up spices for turkey and experience the love when your family bites into its delectable flavor. A word of caution - use sparingly as you don't want to overpower the dish.

Sage A favorite around Thanksgiving, this is the key ingredient for good stuffing. The flavor tends to be on the musky side and goes especially well with fatty meats such as goose and pork. Use it to wake up spices in the brine for your turkey and experience the love when your family bites into your delicious creation.

Parsley Available in two varieties; flat and curly, this herb is wonderful in sauces and stuffing. A nice companion for use as a seasoning for white fish, potatoes, and it also works well with garlic and capers for Italian and French recipes. And when you are searching for a nice garnish for savory dishes, parsley is a safe go-to.

VEGETABLES

If you made the decision to accept my challenge to plant that vegetable garden, this is the perfect list to use as a starting point. Or if you are not quite there yet, this list can also be used as a guide of what to buy fresh when visiting the farmer's market or grocery store. If you are looking to start a vegetable garden, most of these can be started from seeds, which can cut a huge dent in your food budget.

LETTUCES

Mesclun The traditional mix of salad greens originates from the Provence region of Southern France and usually includes chervil, arugula, leafy lettuces and endive; although it is not uncommon for growers to combine a mix of whatever is available. If planting in your own garden, mesclun grows best in early to late spring.

Butterhead Relatively easy to grow, butterhead lettuces are soft, with a buttery-texture whose leaves form into very loose "heads". The flavor is somewhat mild and sweet and tastes best with a mild salad dressing as a way of complementing rather than masking its succulent flavor.

Romaine Romaine lettuce is perhaps the sturdiest of salad greens and is tolerant of heat. The leaves grow upward into a tall head of sturdy leaves with firm ribs that remind you of the leaves of Swiss chard. Mild in flavor, romaine can be used not only in salads, but also on sandwiches and green smoothies.

Arugula With a bit of a bite in flavor, it is also known as rocket. Arugula is an annual plant, which means it has to be planted each growing season. A nice addition to other salad greens, especially spinach, it is a favorite in steak salads. One of my favorite recipes is to use as a bed for grilled fresh peaches with a nice drizzle of balsamic vinegar.

GREENS

Swiss Chard A leafy green vegetable often used in Mediterranean cooking, Swiss chard makes a wonderful sauté when combined with onions or when mixed with other greens such as kale and collards. Very high in antioxidants, this is a good one to add to your list of greens and they are relatively easy to grow from seeds.

Mustards Considered by many to be a super food, this green is jam-packed with vitamins such as flavonoids and Vitamin C. A fall to early winter vegetable, it has a peppery flavor and is a favorite for the southern dinner table. Add to your list of greens, and it is relatively easy to grow.

Collards Very much of a southern staple, collards are slightly bitter and are at their best after the first frost. Harvest times vary depending upon which region of the country you live in. Young tender leaves are best, but more mature leaves are just as tasty, although they take a little longer to cook. Collards are rich in Vitamin K and calcium and the big bonus is they are very low in calories.

Turnip Greens Similar to collards and mustard greens in nutrition, turnip greens however, wins out in Vitamin A. Very flavorful, this particular green goes well with a cornmeal dumpling which is a favorite among southerners.

Kale A member of the cabbage family, kale is actually a type of cabbage that does not form a head. Excellent either cooked or when harvested, the tender leaves are great for a nutrition-packed salad.

Cabbage (Green & Purple) Although there are many varieties of cabbage, the most common are the green and purple, referred to as red cabbage. Cabbage or headed cabbage is a biennial plant but is typically grown as an annual vegetable. Served either cooked or raw in slaws, it is a staple on many lunch and dinner tables.

TOMATOES

Considered to be actual berries, tomatoes come in hundreds of different varieties, ranging from green and yellow to bright red.

Beefsteak At their peak in the summer months, beefsteak tomatoes are deep red in color and very juicy. A perfect choice for salads and sandwiches.

Heirloom My personal preference, heirloom tomatoes, sometimes referred to as heritage tomatoes, is an open-pollinated (non-hybrid) heirloom cultivar of tomato. The appearance is not perfect and often odd in shape. I personally love the variegated colors and interest that they add to fresh dishes.

Grape or ***Cherry*** Very small in size, they come in either yellow or red and the fruit grows in clusters. They are at their peak in mid to late summer. Great as additions to crudité platters or salads.

Roma (Plum Tomato) Plum tomatoes are egg-shaped and are very fleshy compared to other varieties. Peak season for this type of tomato is late summer. They are perfect for sauces, purees, soups and other cooked dishes.

PEPPERS

Red Bell Of the sweet variety, red bell peppers are great for adding not only flavor but eye appeal to dishes. From fire-roasting to stir fry dishes, this pepper is a great addition to your cooking repertoire.

Green Bell A staple for Mexican and Italian dishes, green bell peppers have a variety of uses in the kitchen. Relatively easy to grow and unlike the red bell pepper, the taste is stronger and not as sweet.

Cayenne Often referred to as red hot chili peppers, cayenne peppers are a great way to add spice to meat and vegetable dishes. One great way to preserve its intense flavor is to make up a batch of spicy vinegar which is great drizzled over collards.

Jalapeno Ranging in flavor from medium to very hot, this pepper comes in either deep green to red. Both colors come from the same plant and the final color depends on how long the pepper is left on the vine. Great for additions to chili, sauces and absolutely divine for pickling and using as a table seasoning for collards and cabbage. To cut down on salt, this is a great go-to for adding flavor.

Banana Chiles Small and tapered, ranging in color from yellow to a yellowish green, these are considered to be among the hottest of chili peppers. Great for use in sauces, stews and chiles.

Pablanos A very mild pepper, the color is a very deep green to black. They are great for stuffing or battered up for frying. Poblanos are also referred to as anchos.

BEANS & PEAS

Green Beans Very long and slender, this bean is usually a matte green color. The peak season for harvesting is mid to late summer.

Haricots Verts More slender and smaller than regular green beans, they are at their peak from mid-to-late summer. A beautiful and tasty variety to serve as a side dish.

Black-eyed peas Grown in pods that start off green and once matured, black eyed peas are dotted with brown eyes. Peak season for this southern favorite is summer into fall and is the key ingredient in Hoppin' John.

Snow peas Snow peas are a legume, typically eaten whole in its pod while still unripe. A favorite in stir fry dishes, this can also be eaten raw in salads.

POTATOES

Sweet A southern staple, sweet potatoes are often referred to as yams. This starchy, tuberous vegetable is usually baked, steamed, fried or boiled. And of course, you can't be southern without baking up this delicious tuber in sweet potato pie.

Red Very firm and smooth in texture, this potato ranges from light pink to red with very shallow eyes. Harvested year round, it is moister when very young. Great in soups, mashed, pureed and makes a wonderful salad.

Irish Considered to be the most common among potatoes, these are somewhat round and often misshapen with deep eyes. This potato is best when boiled.

New A personal preference for roasting with herbs and steaming for salads, this potato is typically small, growing no more than 1 to 1/12 inches in diameter.

Russet Fresh in late summer, russet potatoes are best when baked or fried.

OKRA

Common among English-speaking and African countries, this very flavorful vegetable is also a favorite in the Asian community. A must for gumbos, okra is high in fiber and very useful in lowering cholesterol. Okra is best when harvested at two to three inches in length when the flesh is very tender and not too woody and dry.

SQUASH

Yellow Also known as summer squash, they are best when harvested when very young as this is when they are at their tender best. They can also be served raw, as part of a crudite platter, or as a sauté.

Zucchini Zucchini or courgette, a summer squash, is best when harvested very young between 4-6 inches in length. Like yellow squash, it can be served raw or cooked. Also a favorite as a sweet for zucchini bread.

Butternut A vine producing squash, it has a nutty, sweet flavor with a texture similar to pumpkin. Great when roasted, baked in pies or in soup.

Acorn Very popular with gardeners, acorn squash is also referred to as pepper squash. It is harvested in the winter months with a yellow-orange flavor and is sweet in taste.

Carrots Carrots are a root vegetable, usually orange in color, although it also grows in purple, black, red, white, and yellow. A favorite among cooks, it can be eaten raw, used in salads and a wonderful addition to stir fry, in stews and dessert.

ONIONS

Garlic An essential for every good cook, garlic grows by forming a bulb, covered with a white or red-streaked papery skin. Great for use in all kinds of savory dishes as well as roasted or pureed.

Scallions Scallions are typically eaten raw in salads or as an ingredient in cooked dishes. Very popular in Asian dishes.

Pearl Small and oval in shape, they are typically white, yellow or red. They can be pickled, boiled and very popular for stews and braises.

Leeks Long in shape with a white root end and dark green tops, leeks are quite tasty when grilled, braised, steamed, in stews and as the main attraction for a variety of recipes.

Shallots Grown in bunches, shallots are typically available in single bulbs, are light brown with a papery skin, with a white to purple flesh. A popular ingredient for savory dishes.

Spanish A large onion with a yellow to yellow-brown skin, they are milder in flavor than the typical yellow variety. Great for stews, sauces and for braising.

Sweet A white to tan color, the flesh is very sweet. Known as Vidalia, Maui and Walla Walla, these are great in salads, grilled or sautéed.

Yellow Moderately-sized with a yellow-brown color, the skin is papery with a relatively pungent flavor. Generally used in soups, stews, sauces and braises.

Ramps This is a wild leek with small white stem ends with flat green tops. Great when stewed or sautéed.

Chives A perennial plant, chives is common across Europe, Asia, and North America. A favorite for use in butters, as an addition to cream cheese spreads and as an addition to egg dishes.

FRUIT

Strawberries The garden strawberry is a widely-grown hybrid species cultivated around the world for its fruit and loved for its aroma, bright red color, juicy texture, and sweetness. Very popular eaten fresh, frozen, cooked in desserts and canned for jams.

Blueberries Blueberries are perennial flowering plants, producing indigo-colored berries. Blueberries are native to North America. Great when eaten fresh from the bush, in salads, dessert and canned in jams.

IN THE CUPBOARD

This list is a great one to use as a guide to stock your cupboards. These are the basics that will prepare you for almost any recipe. Check for sales and be sure to rotate your stock to avoid using items that are out of date and to achieve the best in flavor.

Kosher Salt
Sea Salt
Black Pepper (coarse ground and whole berries)
Dry Mustard
Dried Herbs
    Oregano
    Basil
    Thyme
    Rosemary
    Sage

Mustards & Condiments
    Yellow
    Brown
    Dijon
    Brown Grain
Vinegars
    White
    Red
    Wine
    Balsamic
    Apple Cider

Oils
    Olive
    Coconut
    Avocado
    Walnut

Dried Beans
    Red
    Navy (also known as white beans)
    Black
    Lentils

Cellar Stock
    Onions (Red, Yellow, Sweet)
    Garlic
    Sweet Potatoes
    Gold Yukon Potatoes
    White Irish Potatoes

THE FRIDGE

Butter
    Unsalted
    European
Dairy
    Cream
    Whole Milk
    Half and Half
    Yogurt and Olive Oil Spreads
    Mayonnaise

Other
    Coconut Milk
    Pepper Sauce

THE FREEZER

Freezers are great to preserve items at the end of the growing season or when meats, fish and produce are on sale. Be sure to use items within a few weeks or months for the best nutritional value and flavor.

"My best days, indeed my most favorite days, will always be Sundays"

SUNDAY SUPPER

There is something pretty special about gathering around the table for Sunday supper, with everyone talking all at once - a reminder of why eating together is key to the making of family.

Keeping one's elbows off the table or reaching over to steal a bite off your cousin's plate is somehow forgiven during Sunday supper. Good manners don't seem to matter as much because being together and sharing in the moment is what is most important.

Sundays are a special time to slow down the pace after a hectic week. A time to cast away the cares of the world around you, kick off your shoes for a bit, allowing your toes to wiggle freely while the goodness of what has been set before you leaves your taste buds squirming with delight.

The idea that it has to be a big production is far from the truth. You can decide how simple or elaborate to make this weekly get-together; although my advice is to keep it simple and instead focus on making the time spent with loved ones the main attraction. After all, years from now, when all that is left is reflection, what will be remembered are the conversations and time spent gathered around the dinner table.

Lemon Skillet Fried Chicken with Whole Cranberry Sauce
Old Fashioned Potato Salad
Spicy Collard Greens
Shrimp Gumbo
Skillet Corn Bread
Short Ribs with Honey & Caramelized Onions
Southern Fish Stew
Lobster Mac 'n Cheese
Cornish Hens with Citrus Garlic Sauce
Perlou Rice (Chicken 'n Rice)
Sweet Potato Casserole with Maple Walnut Topping
Farro with Mushrooms & Shallots
Hearty Chicken Stew with Cumin
Arugula Salad with Grape Tomatoes & Avocado
Rosalie's Yeast Rolls
Chicken Delicious Pot Pie
Red Beans & Rice with Grilled Chicken and Apple Sausage
Smoky Lemon Garlic Cornish Hens

LEMON SKILLET FRIED CHICKEN

WITH WHOLE CRANBERRY SAUCE

Serves 6-8

Sunday suppers and fried chicken go together like Florida sunshine and sudden cloud bursts in the middle of summer. And this recipe is sure to have your family longing for weekends just for a chance to sink their teeth into this all-time southern favorite.

The secret to good fried chicken is a cast iron skillet, or what I use for my recipe, a cast iron pot. If you don't own one, now might be a good time to make this worthwhile investment.

Ingredients

1 whole fryer, cut into parts

1 cup buttermilk

1 ½ teaspoons each: cayenne pepper, coarse ground black pepper, granulated garlic, sweet paprika, Kosher salt, poultry seasoning

1 cup all-purpose flour

Avocado or other vegetable oil for frying

Fresh lemon

Instructions

1. Place fryer parts in a large glass bowl. Pour buttermilk over chicken. Cover bowl with plastic wrap and place in refrigerator to marinate for at least 1 hour.
2. When ready to cook, remove bowl from refrigerator. Pour enough oil into an iron skillet, coming up about half way the pan. Heat on medium until hot. Oil is hot enough when a drop of water dances when dropped in the pan.
3. Meanwhile, put flour, spices and salt in a large plastic zip lock bag. Close bag and shake to thoroughly mix flour and spices together. Using tongs, remove pieces of chicken from bowl, shake off excess buttermilk and add to flour mixture. Shake to coat each chicken piece and add to hot oil. Brown chicken on one side. Turn and cover with a lid to allow chicken to cook through. Do not rush the process.

4. Check chicken for doneness by gently cutting through the thickest part of the chicken and if the juices run clear, it is done.

5. Drain on a plate or pan that has been lined with paper towels. For a nice finish to the chicken and to add an extra burst of flavor, squeeze a little lemon juice over the chicken immediately after removing from skillet while the chicken is piping hot.

6. Serve with a side of Whole Cranberry Sauce (recipe follows), fresh lemon slices and hot pepper sauce.

TIP If you are watching calories, add just enough oil to coat the bottom of the skillet and brown chicken on each side. Transfer to a metal cooling rack placed on a cookie sheet and bake in a hot, 400-degree oven until nice and crispy. To test for doneness, cut into the thickest part of the chicken and if the juices run clear, it is done.

WHOLE CRANBERRY SAUCE

Cranberry Sauce is not just for Thanksgiving or Christmas dinner; which is when most people typically serve it up with their favorite stuffing.

Around our house, you can always find a jar stashed in the fridge to serve with fried chicken, fish or other meats. The sweet, tart flavor is a perfect side dish to lend an unusual note to traditional flavors.

During the holidays, make up extra jars to give as hostess gifts. Not only is it very economical, but your hostess will absolutely love you.

Ingredients

4 cups fresh whole cranberries

1 ½ cups organic sugar

1 cup water

½ teaspoon rose water (you can find this at speciality food stores)

Canning jars

Instructions

1. In a small sauce pot, add water and sugar. Stir. Bring to a slow bowl over medium heat. Add cranberries. Reduce heat and simmer to reduce liquid and thicken; about 10 minutes. Be sure to keep a close eye on the pot to prevent boiling over. Add rose water and stir. Pour cranberries into hot sterilized canning jars and seal.

OLD FASHIONED POTATO SALAD

Serves 8-10

Whether in mid-summer, spring, or as a part of the Christmas holiday meal, every good southern menu has to include potato salad. This recipe is a favorite among my family and I am almost sure it will become a favorite around your house too.

Ingredients

8-10 russet or Yukon gold potatoes

6 large eggs, hard boiled and chopped

Duke's or your favorite mayonnaise, enough to bind the potatoes together

2 tablespoons Sauer's or your favorite yellow mustard

1 cup sweet pickle relish

1 tablespoon fresh dill, chopped

1 teaspoon Kosher Salt

White vinegar

Instructions

1. Peel and cube potatoes. Add to a large pot and add enough cold water to come about two inches above potatoes. Cook until tender. Do not overcook. Drain. Rinse with cold water until cooled. Put potatoes into a large mixing bowl.
2. Toss potatoes with about 3 tbsp. white vinegar. Cover bowl with plastic wrap and refrigerate for at least one hour or overnight.
3. Remove potatoes from refrigerator. Add mustard, dill, salt and pickle relish. Mix. Add enough mayonnaise to bind potatoes. Fold in eggs. Transfer salad into a large serving bowl. Sprinkle with a little paprika. Refrigerate until ready to serve.

SPICY COLLARD GREENS

Serves 8-10

Any southern menu, especially if you are African American, is not complete without a good mess of collard greens on occasion. This traditional vegetable has been a staple of our community for almost as long as we have existed on American soil. Over the years other ethnicities have discovered the nutritional value and flavor of this indigenous staple of the Southern United States and African countries. Very high in calcium, collard greens are a great addition especially if you have family members who are lactose intolerant and need to boost their calcium intake.

This is a spicy version of the traditional recipe, and trust me, you won't miss the bacon.

Ingredients

2 lbs. fresh collards, washed, stems removed and chopped

2 tablespoons finely chopped ginger root

1 large yellow onion, chopped

3 cloves fresh garlic, peeled and finely chopped

1-2 hot cayenne peppers, seeds removed and finely chopped

1 large red bell pepper, chopped

Olive oil

4 tablespoons balsamic vinegar

2 tablespoons raw sugar

Kosher salt and coarse ground black pepper, to taste

Instructions

1. Heat a generous amount of olive oil in a heavy duty pot. Add onions and sauté until transparent. Add garlic and ginger, sauté 2-3 minutes over low heat. Add red bell pepper, cayenne pepper, and sauté until just tender. Add collards, salt, pepper, raw sugar and balsamic sugar. Reduce flame to lowest setting and steam until tender. Do not overcook.

TIP for maximum flavor, avoid adding liquid, however, if necessary add little at a time.

SHRIMP GUMBO

Serves 8-10

This is one of my personal favorites and my family and friends insist on having this on the menu for Christmas dinner. For maximum flavor, I will typically make this dish at least a day ahead of the celebration. The extra day of resting does wonders to helping the ingredients to marry together creating the perfect harmony of delectable flavor. The secret to good gumbo is patience and a good roux; the thickener that makes this dish absolutely divine.

Ingredients

2 lbs. medium shrimp, deveined

1 large green bell pepper, chopped

1 large yellow onion, chopped

4 cloves garlic, chopped

2 stalks celery, chopped

1 tablespoon granulated garlic

Kosher salt, to taste

More Ingredients

Fresh ground black pepper, to taste

1 teaspoon poultry seasoning

1 tablespoon dried thyme, basil and oregano

2 bay leaves

1 18-oz can organic tomatoes

1 stick unsalted butter

¼ cup all-purpose flour

3 cups water

Olive oil

1 cup chopped okra, frozen or fresh

Filé powder

Instructions

1.   Heat a large sauté pan. Add onions, bell pepper, garlic and celery and saute until tender. In a separate heavy-duty pot, add butter and melt. Whisk in flour and cook on low heat, stirring constantly, until mixture thickens and becomes a rich caramel color. This is your roux. Add vegetables to the roux mixture. Add tomatoes, spices and water. Simmer for 10 minutes. Add okra and shrimp. Simmer for 30 minutes on very low heat. Add filé powder just before serving. Perfect served with rice.

SKILLET CORN BREAD

Serves 8-10

A good southern meal simply cannot happen without a nice serving of hot cornbread, preferably slathered with creamy butter. The original family recipe calls for melted butter, but to make it healthier, I took the liberty of substituting avocado oil. And to my pleasant surprise the bread bakes up very light and the flavor is still amazing. The up side, no one will be able to tell the difference.

Ingredients

2 cups stone ground corn meal

1 cup all-purpose flour

1 tablespoon baking powder

1 teaspoon salt

1 teaspoon baking soda

5 tablespoons organic sugar

1 ½ cups buttermilk

2 eggs

¼ cup avocado oil

2 tablespoons unsalted butter

Instructions

1. In a large bowl, sift together, flour, cornmeal, salt, sugar, baking soda. In another bowl, mix together eggs, buttermilk and avocado oil until well-blended. Add egg mixture into flour mixture and mix until just blended. Do not over mix.
2. Melt butter and pour into bottom of a 8x8 baking pan or cast iron skillet. Pour cornbread batter into pan. Bake in 350-degree oven until done. Bread is done when top is nicely browned and toothpick inserted in center comes out clean.

SHORT RIBS

WITH HONEY &
CARAMELIZED ONIONS

Serves 8-10

Short ribs are at their flavorful best when cooked at least a day ahead of serving. Find a good butcher, there are still quite a few around, especially in urban neighborhoods, and have the butcher cut the ribs to the desired length and ask him/her to trim off the excess fat. This recipe is sure to have your family and friends asking for a second helping, so be sure to make enough.

Ingredients

5 lbs. short ribs, remove excess fat and skin

1 large yellow onion, chopped

1 large red onion, chopped

5 cloves fresh garlic, finely chopped

2-3 bay leaves

3 large carrots, chopped

2 tablespoons fresh minced ginger

1 tablespoon smoked paprika

1 ½ tablespoons ground black pepper

¼ cup low-sodium soy sauce

¼ cup pure honey

½-¾ cups port wine

2 tablespoons olive oil

Instructions

1. Preheat oven to 325 degrees.
2. Prepare short ribs by cutting away all excess fat. Season short ribs with black pepper. Heat a large Dutch oven or heavy duty pot over medium heat until hot. Add enough olive oil to cover bottom of pot. Add seasoned short ribs and brown on both sides.
3. Transfer short ribs to a platter and set aside. Add onions and cook slowly until caramelized, about 3-4 minutes. Cook on low heat to avoid burning. Add additional oil if necessary to prevent burning. Add carrots and ginger. Cook for 2 minutes. Add port wine and cook until a slight glaze appears. Return short ribs to the pot. Add remaining ingredients and bring to a gentle boil. Transfer pot to preheated oven and bake until completely done. Be sure to check occasionally and add a little water if necessary to prevent burning.

SOUTHERN FISH STEW

Serves 6-10

Some of my fondest memories of growing up was the smell of fresh fish stew wafting through the house. With someone in our family bringing home a fresh catch at least once a week, it was expected that a good fish stew was certain to be on the menu. Making stew for my husband and kids always takes me back to my childhood memories. This recipe can be adjusted to use whatever fish you have on hand; just make sure that whatever fish is used that it is firm and will hold up when added to the stew.

Ingredients

2 stalks celery, chopped

1 large green bell pepper, chopped

1 large yellow onion, chopped

2 cans organic tomatoes or 1lb. fresh- chopped

2 tablespoons tomato paste

Fresh garlic, basil, oregano, thyme

Olive oil

Salt and pepper, to taste

More Ingredients

1 lb. Red snapper filets

12 oz. clam juice

1 lb. shrimp

2 tablespoons unsalted butter

2 tablespoons all-purpose flour

1 teaspoon red pepper flakes

6-8 Yukon gold potatoes, peeled and diced

2 ears fresh corn, kernels removed from cob

Liquid smoke or bacon

Instructions

1. Drain tomatoes, reserving liquid. Add tomatoes to a large baking sheet. During growing season, use fresh meaty tomatoes such as plum. Add herbs and toss. Drizzle with 2 tablespoons olive oil. Roast tomatoes in a preheated 350 degree oven for 20 minutes. Remove from oven.
2. Heat a large heavy duty pot and add enough olive oil to coat the bottom. Sauté celery, onion and bell pepper until just tender. Add flour and stir until slightly cooked. Add roasted tomatoes and reserved tomato liquid and stir. Add 2 cups hot water and 12 oz. clam juice or fish stock. Add potatoes and corn. Simmer for 10 minutes. Add clams, red snapper and shrimp. Cover pot. Simmer for 15-20 minutes. If desired, add ½ teaspoon liquid smoke.

TIP If using bacon, fry bacon until done to render (melt) the fat. Remove from pot and sauté vegetables in bacon fat. This is especially good if made a day in advance to allow the flavors to meld. Be sure to cool completely before placing in refrigerator.

LOBSTER MAC 'N CHEESE

Serves 6-8

This recipe landed me an ambush by Al Roker and an appearance on the Today Show. Served each year as a part of my Thanksgiving and Christmas menu, this mouthwatering dish can be served as a side, or it works perfectly as the main attraction when accompanied by a green salad or vegetable. For the pasta, I use a whole grain variety which adds a rich and nutty flavor to the dish and the bonus, it is healthier for you. To save time, make ahead and bake just before dinner until hot and bubbly.

Ingredients

1 16 oz. box good whole grain elbow macaroni

2 cans Carnation evaporated milk or 8 oz. half and half &
8 oz. whole milk (room temperature)

1 lb. good medium or sharp cheddar cheese, grated

1 stick butter, unsalted

2 tablespoons all-purpose flour

1 teaspoon kosher salt

1 teaspoon coarse ground black pepper

1 lb. cooked lobster meat, chopped into chunks

1 ½ teaspoons dry mustard

Topping: ½ cup bread crumbs, 1 tablespoon butter

Instructions

1. Fill a large pot with water and bring to a boil. Add entire contents of box of macaroni and cook until just tender. Do not overcook. Drain.
2. In a large sauce pan, add butter and melt. Whisk in flour and cook for one minute, stirring constantly. Add milk, continuing to whisk until well-blended. Mix in dry mustard, salt and pepper. Add cheese and stir to create a medium-thick sauce. If too thick, add a little more milk. Blend in lobster meat. Mix together pasta and cheese sauce. Pour into lightly-oiled baking dish.
3. To make topping, melt 1 tablespoon butter in a small sauté pan. Add bread crumbs and mix until completely coated. Add buttered bread crumbs to top of macaroni and cheese. Bake in a 350-degree oven until bubbly.

CORNISH HENS

WITH CITRUS GARLIC SAUCE

Serves 4

This dish is not only relatively easy to make, but it makes for an elegant presentation. The combination of orange and lemon makes this dish sing! If Meyer's lemons are available, use these instead for a flavor that is out of this world.

Ingredients

2 fresh Cornish hens

4 cloves colossal garlic, thinly sliced

Fresh rosemary and thyme

Juice from two lemons

Juice from 1 orange

Zest from 1 lemon and 1 orange

Kosher salt

Fresh ground black pepper

Olive oil

Instructions

1. Preheat oven to 350 degrees. Split Cornish hens in half, cleaning the insides of the birds completely. Season with salt and pepper.
2. Heat a large sauté pan and add a generous amount of olive oil; enough to coat the pan. Place hens skin side down in the pan and sear until browned on one side. Turn the hens and add sliced garlic. Cover hens with a lid that fits securely on pan. Place pan with hens in oven and bake for 25 minutes.
3. Remove pan from oven. Add rosemary, thyme, orange and lemon juice and zests. Return to oven and continue cooking until liquid thickens and reduces. Baste hens in sauce periodically to add the flavor of the drippings to the hens.

PERLOU RICE

(CHICKEN 'N RICE)

Serves 8-10

This classic southern dish is still a favorite for my family especially during the Thanksgiving and Christmas holiday season. When making this dish, I always think about my Aunt Martha, who made this dish to perfection. Not many people know this but her name was actually Martha Stewart! No, not the famed one! Actually, my aunt Martha had the name first since she would have been in her eighties had she lived.

It is a nice side dish or can be served up as the main course with vegetables and a salad. The key to this dish is patience and lots of seasoning. I have changed the original recipe by cooking the chicken a day in advance and storing overnight in the refrigerator to remove the fat. Trust me, when it comes to flavor, the only thing missing from this recipe is the fat.

Ingredients

6 chicken breasts

1 large yellow onion, diced

1 carrot, chopped

1 green bell pepper, diced

1 bay leaf

1 stalk celery, diced

Kosher salt, 1 tablespoon

1 tablespoon granulated garlic

Fresh Ground Black Pepper, 1 teaspoon

Instructions

1. Put chicken pieces in a large heavy duty pot and cover with cold water about six inches above chicken. Add chopped vegetables and bay leaf. Place on stove top and bring to low boil and lower heat to very low. Cover with a tight lid and cook until chicken is completely done, about 1 hour. Turn off stove and allow to cool completely. When cool, store in refrigerator overnight.
2. The following day, remove chicken from the refrigerator and skim off any solid fat that has formed on the top. Take chicken from the pot and remove skin and bones from chicken. Shred chicken breasts into small pieces. Heat up broth and vegetables. Pour through a fine strainer to separate broth from vegetables. Discard vegetables.
3. Add chicken and 2 ½ cups of the strained broth to a Dutch oven. Add 1 ½ cup brown rice. Stir to mix. Bring to a boil and then lower heat to very low. Cook until completely done. I normally will transfer the pot to the oven to allow the rice to finish cooking. When done, use a fork to separate the grains immediately.

SWEET POTATO CASSEROLE

WITH MAPLE WALNUT TOPPING

Serves 8-10

In late summer to early fall, I look forward to digging up these red beauties from my vegetable garden.

Sweet potatoes are a staple in most traditional southern homes and there are as many ways to prepare them as there are individual tastes. Whether prepared sweet or savory, sweet potatoes are the perfect base to creating delicious recipes for your table.

My family looks forward to this dish at Christmas and Thanksgiving. It is the ultimate side dish as a complement to our traditional ox tails, short ribs, or jerk turkey. And because it is packed with nutrition, it can also be served as a main course with a side of green vegetables.

Ingredients

3 cups mashed baked sweet potatoes

1/3 cup organic granulated sugar

¼ cup unsalted butter, melted

1 teaspoon vanilla extract

1 teaspoon nutmeg

2 large eggs, slightly beaten

½ cup coconut cream

Topping

1/3 cup melted butter

1 cup brown sugar

½ cup all purpose flour

1 cup roughly-chopped maple walnuts

Instructions

1. Bake 2-3 large sweet potatoes, wrapped in aluminum foil, in a 350-degree oven until done. Peel potatoes and mash with a fork. Measure out 3 cups cooked potatoes into a large mixing bowl. Add sugar, butter, vanilla, eggs and coconut cream. Combine.
2. Spoon potato mixture into a lightly-oiled 9X13 inch baking pan.
3. Add maple walnut topping on top of potato mixture.
4. Bake for 25 minutes in a preheated 350-degree oven until crunchy on top and potato mixture is bubbling hot.

Maple Walnuts

2 cups walnut halves

½ cup maple syrup

⅓ cup brown sugar

Instructions

1. Preheat oven to 350 degrees.
2. Add all ingredients to a small sauce pan. Cook over medium heat for 2 minutes; until bubbling. Add parchment paper to a small baking sheet. Pour walnuts onto baking sheet and spread out walnuts to form single layer. Bake for 20 minutes or until slightly brown. Be sure to watch closely to avoid burning. Remove pan from oven when done and set aside to cool. Once cooled, break apart nuts using a wooden spoon. In addition to topping, these also make a wonderful snack or packaged as a hostess gift during the holidays.

FARRO

WITH MUSHROOMS & SHALLOTS

Serves 6-8

I love when I discover a new ingredient that is not only tasty but also packed with good nutrition. Farro is very versatile, excellent as a side dish, main attraction, and it has all the flavor you need to create an amazing salad. When combined with mushrooms, this hearty grain makes an easy pass for fine, as in fine dining, especially when paired with a glass of your favorite red or white wine.

Ingredients

1 medium yellow onion, chopped

6 cloves garlic, chopped

2 cups farro, cooked in boiling water

3 shallots, chopped

½ lbs. sliced Cremini mushrooms

Olive oil

Kosher salt and freshly ground black pepper

¾ cup white wine

Grated parmesan

2 tablespoons butter

Instructions

1. Cook farro in 4 cups of salted boiling water for 10-15 minutes or until tender. Heat a large sauté pan and coat generously with olive oil. Add 2 tablespoons butter to pan, along with onions, shallots and garlic and sauté until just tender. Add mushrooms and continue to sauté until tender. Add wine and cook to reduce liquid until it becomes slightly thickened. Drain farro and add to vegetable mixture. Toss. Top with parmesan cheese.

TIP for a fuller flavor add 2 tablespoons of cream or coconut milk to vegetable mixture.

HEARTY CHICKEN STEW

WITH CUMIN

Serves 6-8

The cold winter months usually mean an increased craving for comfort food. Typically when we think of comfort food, we imagine the pounds that come along with a lot of the traditional recipes.

One way to keep the calories at bay is to reduce or when possible, eliminate the obvious fat and add flavor through unusual and flavorful spices and herbs.

This chicken stew recipe uses one of the cheaper cuts of the chicken and the calories are very much on the good side. The addition of cumin makes this dish oh so flavorful and the full flavor helps to keep the appetite in check. You can use your crock pot for this dish, but I prefer my trusty Dutch oven to render a richer flavor.

Ingredients

10 chicken legs, lower portion of leg removed

1 large yellow onion diced

8 cloves garlic, chopped

2 teaspoons cumin

Kosher Salt and fresh ground black pepper, to taste

½ cup chicken stock

8 medium red potatoes, peeled and quartered

Instructions

1. Preheat oven to 350-degrees. Remove lower portion of chicken legs with a meat cleaver. Remove skin and all visible fat. Place in a large Dutch oven. Add remaining ingredients. Cover with lid. Bake for about 1½ hours making sure to check after 45 minutes, adding a little water or broth if needed.

ARUGULA SALAD

WITH GRAPE TOMATOES & AVOCADO

Serves 4-6

One of the things I love about growing my own food are the endless choices I find just walking outside to my vegetable garden. When choosing what to plant in my vegetable garden, I usually plant no less than 8-10 different kinds of salad greens. While growing up lettuce was overwhelmingly of the iceberg variety. I was somewhat fortunate however, that I had a grandmother who, by today's standards, would have been considered a gourmet cook. She was unafraid to do things outside of the norm. I imagine I can attribute my curiosity for food to her. This recipe for arugula salad is one of my family's favorites. A little bitey in taste, it works well as a side salad or as a dinner salad with a piece of grilled fish or chicken. And if you really want to go all out, top off your salad with a nice grilled porterhouse steak. Now that is what you call real good.

Ingredients

Arugula greens

½ lb. cherry or grape tomatoes, halved

2 ripe, but firm, avocados cut into chunks

Garlic balsamic vinaigrette

Garlic Balsamic Vinaigrette

¼ cup balsamic vinegar

2 cloves crushed fresh garlic

1 cup Extra Virgin oil

½ teaspoon Kosher salt

½ teaspoon coarse ground black pepper

1 tablespoon dijon mustard

1 tablespoon cold water

1 teaspoon honey

Instructions

1. Add arugula, tomatoes and avocado to a large bowl. Toss.
2. Add all ingredients for Vinaigrette with the exception of olive oil to a large mixing bowl. Whisk together ingredients until well blended. Slowly drizzle olive oil into mixture, steadily whisking as you drizzle, until mixture thickens. Refrigerate until ready to serve.
3. Drizzle salad with vinaigrette.

ROSALIE'S YEAST ROLLS

Serves 8-10

I will always remember the Christmas when my nephew brought his wife and her family to visit with us from the Bahamas. I had met his wife some years earlier and although I found her at the time to be a real sweetheart, it became evident during that visit that he had indeed found a person of incredible character to journey with him through life.

I immediately bonded with his mother in-law, Rosalie, who while I busied myself in the kitchen on Christmas Eve, thought nothing of coming downstairs to dig in by making up a batch of her melt-in-your-mouth yeast rolls. As I am writing this, I can still taste the tender, mouthwatering flavor of the rolls that graced our table that year. Thankfully, I requested the recipe a short time later after their visit, because a couple years after meeting her, she passed away.

And so, Rosalie, this is my dedication to you for all the love you poured into Natalie, who is now sharing that love in so many special ways and for the wonderful memory you left me and my family.

Ingredients

10 cups all-purpose flour

1 stick unsalted butter

1 cup shortening

1 ½ - 2 cups coconut milk

2 ½ tablespoons dry active yeast

3-4 tablespoons organic sugar

1 cup lukewarm water

Instructions

1. Add yeast, water and sugar in a small bowl and mix until well blended. Allow to rest until yeast begins to bubble and becomes active.
2. Add coconut milk, butter and salt to a small pot. Heat until hot, but not boiling. Turn off flame and cool to room temperature.
3. In a large mixing bowl, cut shortening and butter into flour until like small peas. Mix coconut milk into yeast mixture, blend into flour mixture, knead until smooth and dough no longer sticks to hands. Transfer to a large bowl that has been lightly oiled.
4. Cover with plastic wrap and place in a warm area to rise until doubled. Remove plastic wrap. Punch down dough and let rise again.
5. Shape dough into 3-inch rolls, placing on a lightly-oiled baking sheet. Brush rolls with egg wash. Let rise to about double in size. Brush with an egg wash. Bake in 350 degree oven for 15 – 20 minutes. Remove from oven. Brush with melted butter.

TIP For the most amazing breakfast rolls, knead in brown sugar, raisins and cinnamon. Shape into rolls. Brush with an egg wash or melted butter and bake.

CHICKEN DELICIOUS POT PIE

Serves 8-10

My recipe for chicken pot pie is a family favorite for Sunday supper. Growing up in the south you could always count on dishes with chicken, beef, pork, or sometimes seafood, baked under a tender, flaky crust with whatever available vegetables from the garden.

I have given the traditional recipe a bit of a twist, using lots of herbs and roasting the vegetables in the pan with the chicken to add rich notes to the flavor. I also use corn starch as a thickener as opposed to the traditional southern flour thickener to give it a lighter texture.

If you are pressed for time, you can always make ahead of time and heat in the oven prior to serving.

Ingredients

1 large roasting chicken

Kosher salt, to taste

Coarse ground black pepper

Dried or fresh thyme and oregano

Dried basil

½ each, ground fennel and celery seed (grind in a mortar pestle)

2 bay leaves

5-6 fresh carrots, scrubbed and peeled

1 cup frozen baby green peas

8 garlic cloves

White pearl onions

½ large lemon

2 ½ cups chicken broth

2 tablespoons corn starch

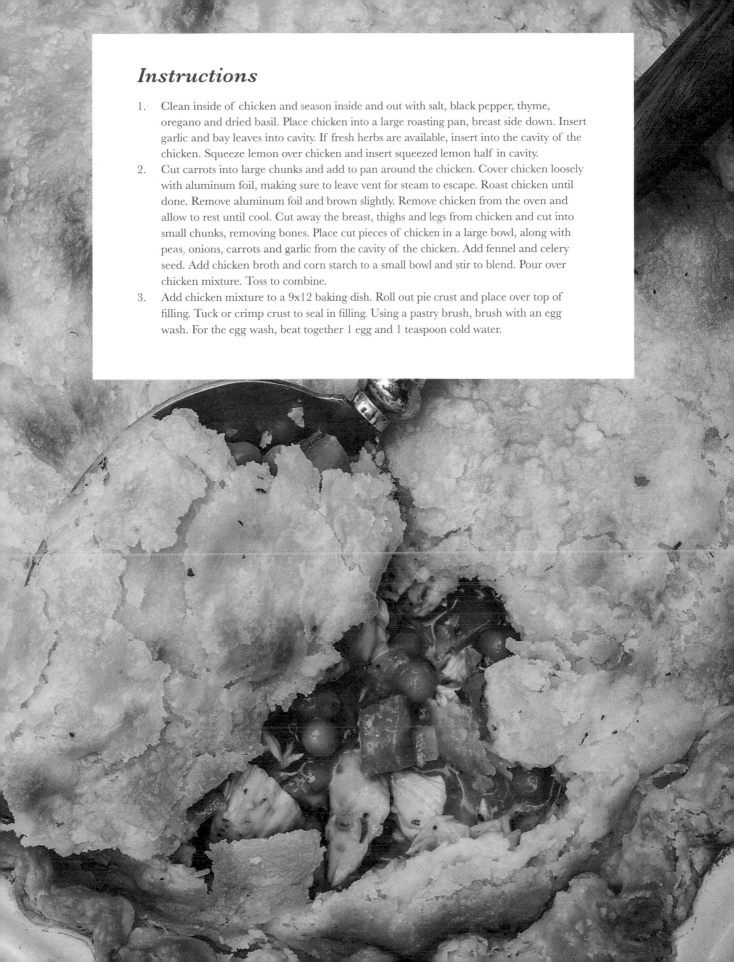

Instructions

1. Clean inside of chicken and season inside and out with salt, black pepper, thyme, oregano and dried basil. Place chicken into a large roasting pan, breast side down. Insert garlic and bay leaves into cavity. If fresh herbs are available, insert into the cavity of the chicken. Squeeze lemon over chicken and insert squeezed lemon half in cavity.

2. Cut carrots into large chunks and add to pan around the chicken. Cover chicken loosely with aluminum foil, making sure to leave vent for steam to escape. Roast chicken until done. Remove aluminum foil and brown slightly. Remove chicken from the oven and allow to rest until cool. Cut away the breast, thighs and legs from chicken and cut into small chunks, removing bones. Place cut pieces of chicken in a large bowl, along with peas, onions, carrots and garlic from the cavity of the chicken. Add fennel and celery seed. Add chicken broth and corn starch to a small bowl and stir to blend. Pour over chicken mixture. Toss to combine.

3. Add chicken mixture to a 9x12 baking dish. Roll out pie crust and place over top of filling. Tuck or crimp crust to seal in filling. Using a pastry brush, brush with an egg wash. For the egg wash, beat together 1 egg and 1 teaspoon cold water.

RED BEANS & RICE

WITH GRILLED CHICKEN
& APPLE SAUSAGE

Serves 6-8

Quick and easy, but oh so good is the best way to describe this dish. There are several varieties of organic, uncured (which mean no nitrates) sausages available at most food markets. If your favorite market does not carry them, it is as simple as asking them to add it to their shelves.

Ingredients

2 cups cooked dried red beans

3 cups cooked brown rice

4 organic chicken apple sausages

1 green bell pepper, chopped

1 medium yellow onion, chopped

1 can whole kernel corn or 2 ears fresh corn, kernels removed

3 cloves fresh garlic, minced

3 tablespoons olive oil

4 tablespoons tomato paste

2 teaspoons chili powder

Kosher Salt

Coarse Ground black pepper

Instructions

1. Add olive oil to a hot heavy duty pot. Add onion and sauté until tender. Add green bell pepper and sauté for 2 minutes. Add garlic and sauté for an additional minute. Add an additional 1 tablespoon olive oil and tomato paste. Stir until it glistens. Add brown rice. Mix well. Add in corn and red beans. Mix well. Add seasonings and a little water. Heat through.
2. Grill sausage until done. Remove from grill. Cut into slices and add to beans and rice mixture and toss to incorporate.
3. Serve with salsa and hot pepper sauce.

TIP In a pinch substitute canned beans

SMOKY LEMON GARLIC CORNISH HENS

Serves 6-8

Around our house, Easter means dining at home and inviting a few friends over for Sunday supper to celebrate our faith and to usher in the new season. I especially love creating new recipes to add to the celebration.

This recipe for Smoky Lemon Garlic Cornish Hens with a touch of honey is sure to please even the most finicky eater around your table. The combination of savory, tangy and sweet for this Cornish Hen recipe is a delightful symphony of flavors that will not only tantalize your taste buds, but will also leave you satisfied.

Depending on where you purchase, you can usually find cornish hens at a reasonable price. To determine how many to purchase, calculate $\frac{1}{2}$ hen per adult and $\frac{1}{4}$ per child. And by all means, throw in a couple of extras for a second helping.

Ingredients

4 Fresh Cornish Hens

Juice of 2 large lemons

1 lemon cut into quarters

1 tablespoon each dried – thyme, basil, oregano, rosemary (crushed)

1 tablespoon fresh ground black pepper

4 tablespoons honey

3 tablespoons butter

1 teaspoon liquid smoke

$1/4$ cup soy sauce

4 large garlic cloves

1 $1/2$ dozen petite red potatoes, scrubbed

Instructions

1. Place Cornish hens in a large ovenproof baking dish. Tie legs together and tuck under wings.
2. Insert $1/4$ lemon and 1 large clove garlic inside cavity of each hen. Place potatoes in a bowl and season with one half of the herbs and 2 tablespoons olive oil. Add to the pan placing around the hens. Cover loosely with aluminum foil and bake for 30 minutes.
3. In a small sauce pan, add herbs, lemon juice black pepper, honey, butter, liquid smoke and soy sauce. Bring to a simmer over a low flame, stirring for 5 minutes. Remove from heat. Remove hens from oven and baste with soy sauce mixture.
4. Return to oven and bake an additional 10 minutes. Remove from oven and repeat basting and baking process for an additional 20 minutes or until hens are done. Test for doneness by inserting a fork at the thickest part of the hen between the leg and thigh. If the liquid runs clear, the hens are done.

TIP do not add salt to hens as soy sauce is high in sodium. If you are on a sodium restricted diet, choose one with low sodium.

"Greet each new day with
a grateful heart"

MORNING
SUNSHINE

It is a known fact that breakfast is the most important meal of the
day; a time to fuel your body for the day ahead. Growing up, it was the smell
of bacon wafting throughout the house giving you a big wake-up hug. Over
the years, I have leaned more toward healthier options, such as uncured
turkey bacon or my homemade chicken sausages. That is not to say that if
traditional bacon is what your family prefers that you should not indulge, but
as with all things do it in moderation. This collection of recipes are some of
our favorites and just enough to inspire your breakfast table.

✳

Sweet Potato Biscuits
Apple Bacon Tart
Baked Eggs with Fresh Herbs
Honey Walnut Wheat Bread
Cranberry Scones
Cheddar Omelet with Smoked Salmon & Chives
Strawberry Lavender Jam
Luscious Peach Butter
Flapjacks
Floral Essence Strawberry Muffins
Spicy Shrimp with Parmesan Grits
Baby Spinach Sauté with Fresh Garlic

✳

SWEET POTATO BISCUITS

Serves 6-10

I am a bread-lover! And as a descendant of some of most amazing biscuit makers on the planet, biscuits are among my favorite breads to eat. There is an art to making biscuits, and after years of trial and error during my young adult years, I managed to perfect this family recipe to a decent level of respectability. Sunday morning breakfasts and biscuits are the things dreams are made of. And this recipe for sweet potato biscuits will certainly make all of your dreams come true.

Ingredients

1 cup left over sweet potato pie mixture

2 cups all-purpose flour

½ cup shortening

4 tablespoons unsalted butter

1 cup buttermilk

2 tablespoons baking powder

½ teaspoon salt

½ teaspoon baking soda

zest of 1 lemon

Instructions

1. Sift flour, baking powder, salt, baking soda in a large mixing bowl. Cut in shortening and butter until mixture is the size of small peas. Be sure to leave large chunks of butter throughout mixture. Add sweet potato filling to flour mixture, tossing lightly making sure not to over mix. Add buttermilk, stirring with fork just enough to bind. Press dough together to form a ball, being careful not to work the dough too much. Turn onto a floured surface. Roll out dough to 2-inch thickness. Cut dough using a round cookie cutter. Add to a lightly greased cookie sheet. Brush tops of biscuits with a little melted butter. Bake in a preheated 350-degree oven until done.

APPLE BACON TART

Serves 8

If you are a die-hard bacon lover, you are going to love the marrying together of apple and bacon in this delectable savory tart recipe. It is especially good when apples are fresh from the orchard.

A great dish to serve up for breakfast, brunch or even a lite supper.

Ingredients

8 slices slightly under-cooked bacon, chopped

2 large Granny Smith apples, peeled, cored and sliced

¼ cup crumbled bleu cheese

1 yellow onion, chopped and caramelized

3 cloves chopped garlic, sautéed

Toasted chopped walnuts

Cayenne pepper

2 tablespoons honey

2 Tablespoons brown sugar

Baked pie crust

Instructions

1. In a large sauté pan, add 2 tablespoons olive oil. Sauté sliced apples in pan and cook until just tender. Add brown sugar and stir until caramelized.
2. In another pan, sauté chopped onions until caramelized, add garlic and continue cooking until tender.
3. Add ingredients to baked pie shell by layering beginning with apples, onion/garlic mixture, sliced bacon, bleu cheese and cayenne pepper. Drizzle with honey.
4. Cover loosely with aluminum foil, being careful to leave edges loose to allow steam to escape. Bake for approximately 10 minutes. Remove foil and bake an additional 5 minutes. Remove from oven and allow to rest for 10 minutes. Serve.

BAKED EGGS

WITH FRESH HERBS

Serves 4

They say necessity is the mother of invention and it was out of sheer
necessity that I created this recipe while prepping breakfast for a full house at
my former bed & breakfast inn. This recipe can be baked until almost done
ahead of time and placed in the oven to finish just before serving. Vary the
recipe by adding fresh spinach, mushrooms or precooked ham or bacon or
your favorite filling.

Ingredients

2 cloves chopped garlic

1 tablespoon sun dried tomatoes

1 teaspoon fresh chopped herbs (basil, thyme, oregano)

Kosher salt and coarse black pepper, to taste

2 teaspoons melted butter, add ½ teaspoon to each gratin dish

1 teaspoon olive oil, add ½ teaspoon to each gratin dish

4 eggs, slightly beaten

Instructions

1. Add chopped garlic, tomatoes, butter and olive oil to buttered gratin dishes. Place in preheated 350 degree oven for 5 minutes. Beat eggs slightly, add herbs. Pour into gratin dishes and with a fork gently mix. Return to oven and bake to desired doneness, but do not overcook. Top with a grating of parmesan cheese if desired.

TIP for sunny side up, add one whole egg to dish and bake for a couple of minutes.

HONEY WALNUT WHEAT BREAD

Makes 4 loaves

Nothing makes an okay meal exceptional like good, homemade bread. As the former owner of a restaurant and bakery cafe, one of the things I learned as a restauranteur was in order to make the dining experience memorable for my guests, it was important to begin the meal with very good, warm bread, and end with an exceptional dessert.

This was the case too while growing up. Every meal for as far back as I can remember was always served with fresh bread and I have continued this family tradition throughout the years.

In my own dining experiences, when visiting restaurants, it was the bread that helped to set the stage for the rest of the meal. This recipe is one that I love because of its versatility. It can be served for dinner, it makes a great sandwich and the croutons made from this bread will turn any soup or salad into heaven on a plate. If you find this batch to be too much for your family, it also freezes well for later use.

Ingredients

2 cups heavy cream

2 cups whole milk

4 tablespoons unsalted butter

4 teaspoons kosher salt

1 tablespoons organic sugar

1 tablespoon honey

¾ cup chopped walnuts

6 cups coarse whole wheat flour

1 cup oatmeal flour

More Ingredients

2 cups all-purpose flour

4 ½ teaspoons active dry yeast

1 cup lukewarm water

Instructions

1. In small bowl mix water and yeast together. Whisk lightly until blended.
2. In large sauce pan, add cream, milk, butter, sugar, honey and salt. Scald by heating until bubbles form around edges. Cool to lukewarm. Add yeast mixture to milk mixture in a large mixing bowl of a stand mixer.
3. After adding flours to mixing bowl, knead using a stand mixer, fitted with the dough hook attachment, for 3 minutes. Transfer to a large lightly-oiled bowl. Cover and allow to rise until double in size. Divide in quarters and place in lightly-oiled loaf pans.
4. Brush with an egg wash and bake in a 350 degree oven for 35-40 minutes or until done. To test for doneness, lightly tap bread on top and listen for a hollow sound or insert a skewer in the center. Skewer should slide in and out of bread smoothly.

CRANBERRY SCONES

Makes 24 scones

While growing up it was not unusual around our house to see "church ladies" gathered in my grandmother's living room sipping tea and eating tea cakes while taking care of church business. The truth is because Florida is hot most months out of the year, it was also likely that the tea they were sipping was iced rather than hot.

What I loved most was hearing the conversation back and forth and the laughter that made for such good fellowship. I brought this tradition with me into my adulthood and each year I share this experience with friends during my annual garden tea party.

This recipe for scones is a favorite of my husband who is not much of a tea drinker.

It was also a signature at my former bed and breakfast inn where afternoon tea was a highlight for our guests. One of my favorite memories of the inn was a special visit from Lady Annabelle Fairfax from England who, when served tea, shared that our scones were better than anything she had ever experienced at home which is known for their tradition of high tea.

Whether for tea or for breakfast, this delectable scone recipe is certain to become a favorite with your family.

Ingredients

12 oz. firm butter, cut into pieces

⅔ cup organic sugar

5 tablespoons baking powder

1 teaspoon baking soda

¾ teaspoon salt

6 cups all-purpose flour

2 tablespoons orange zest, fresh

1 cup fresh or frozen cranberries

2 cups buttermilk, plus 2 tablespoons fresh orange juice

Instructions

1. In a large mixing bowl of a stand mixer, combine butter, 3 cups of the flour, baking powder, baking soda, sugar and salt. Using the paddle attachment, at the lowest speed, blend until thoroughly incorporated to the size of peas. Add orange zest, remaining flour and cranberries. Add the buttermilk, pouring slowly and mix until the dough pulls away from the sides of the bowl. Do not over work the dough.

2. Sprinkle a work area with flour, just enough to cover the surface. Place dough on top and roll out the dough to ¾ inch thickness. Cut into rounds. Place on a cookie sheet that has been slightly buttered. Brush with an egg wash. Bake in an oven that has been preheated to 350 degrees until golden brown. Remove onto a cooling rack to cool. Dust with powdered sugar just before serving. Serve with clotted cream and a very good fruit preserve. My personal favorite is orange marmalade.

CHEDDAR OMELET

WITH SMOKED SALMON & CHIVES

Serves 4-6

Southern people love cheese, and not just a little cheese. Although I honor my southern roots, I try to make healthy adjustments to most traditional recipes without skimping on flavor. This recipe adds the full flavor of smoked salmon and chives resulting in decadence that you are going to love. And I promise, you will not miss the extra cheese.

Ingredients

6 large eggs

2 tablespoons unsalted butter

4 tablespoons half and half

¼ cup shredded sharp cheddar cheese

Smoked Salmon, about 2 oz.

Coarse ground black pepper

Snipped chives

Instructions

1. Heat a large skillet on medium heat until hot. Meanwhile, beat eggs completely until lemon-colored adding half and half. Add butter to skillet and melt until bubbly. Be careful not to burn.
2. Add beaten eggs to skillet and with a spatula move eggs gently from sides of pan to middle. When eggs become just set, not done, add cheddar cheese, smoked salmon, black pepper and chives. Immediately place skillet in a preheated 350 degree oven. Bake until desired doneness making sure not to overcook.
3. Remove pan from oven and transfer to serving plate, folding the omelet in the process to close.

TIP Do not add salt without tasting. Sharp cheddar and smoked salmon are both very salty and should provide more than enough flavor.

STRAWBERRY LAVENDER JAM

Makes 1 pint

When I get a craving for homemade croissants or for something extra special on my morning biscuits or toast, my next move is make up a batch of a very good jam to slather over the rich flaky layers for the ultimate culinary experience.

This jam is very simple to make and the perfect way to salvage those berries that you can't manage to eat before having to toss into the trash. It takes about 15 minutes to make and it can be stored in the refrigerator for weeks. I must admit, that I am not sure exactly how many weeks, because for some reason it never lasts around our house. And the addition of fresh lavender blossoms sends the flavor way over the top.

Ingredients

2 cups fresh strawberries, washed and hulled

1 cup organic sugar

½ teaspoon fresh or dried lavender florets

Instructions

1. Cut strawberries into quarters. Add strawberries, sugar and lavender to a medium sauce pan. Place on a medium burner and heat until mixture begins to bubble. Lower heat and cook until berries become slightly tender. Using a hand masher, mash berries until the consistency of a rough puree. Continue to cook until mixture thickens and the back of a metal spoon inserted comes out coated.
2. Remove from stove and spoon into sterilized canning jars and seal. If desired, store in refrigerator or jam can also be frozen in a plastic container designed for the freezer.

LUSCIOUS PEACH BUTTER

Makes 6 pints

As an ode to my grandmother, not a summer passes without a day of making peach butter. During the summer, you would find her making all kinds of preserves, butters, canned vegetables and pickles. And you never visited our home without leaving with one of her goodies from the canning shelf. I have continued this tradition of a care package, which very often means flower bulbs, fresh vegetables or a cutting of fresh flowers from my garden. This recipe is absolutely wonderful slathered on homemade biscuits, croissants or toast; preferably whole grain, for an extra kick of nutty crunchiness.

Ingredients

4-5 lbs. fresh very ripe peaches

2 ½ teaspoons ground cinnamon

1 teaspoon nutmeg

Juice and rind of 1 large lemon

organic sugar

Instructions

1. Peel, pit and cut peaches into large chunks. Place in a heavy-duty pot and bring to a slow boil in their own juice. DO NOT ADD WATER. Immediately reduce heat to simmer and cook until peaches are completely tender. Place peaches, minus juice, in a food processor and blend until smooth. Reserve juice to make peach syrup for luscious pancakes.

2. Transfer peaches to a heavy duty aluminum pan, measuring as you do so.

3. For each cup of peaches, add ¼ cup organic cane sugar. Stir in spices and lemon juice. Cover pan and place in a preheated 325 degree oven on the middle rack and bake for about three hours until mixture becomes very thick.

4. Ladle peaches into hot, clean, sterilized canning jars (sterilize for 20 minutes in boiling hot water). Seal loosely, making sure to clean away any fruit that might have spilled along the sides of the rim. Add lid to jars and seal but not overly tight. Place jars in a canning pot with water about half way up around jars and cook for 10 minutes to destroy any possible bacteria and to seal jars. Remove jars from pot. Using a clean cloth, screw on lids as tight as you can, invert and allow to cool. Once cooled, turn jars upright. If seal pops while cooling, repeat process. Test the seal by gently pressing the top of the lid with your finger. If the lid pops, it is not sealed.

5. Store butter in a cool dark place until ready to use.

FLAPJACKS

Serves 4-6

One of my fondest memories of growing up is the smell of flapjacks and bacon wafting through the house on Saturday morning. The distinct smell of molasses, the sweet ingredient, in this recipe can also be substituted with honey. Warning, be sure to prepare to eat a nice stack of these and then a nap afterwards. Or better yet, take a nice brisk walk and a stroll around the garden before eating to get rid of some of the extra calories.

Ingredients

2 cups all-purpose flour

*1 cup old fashioned oatmeal flour

4 tablespoons old-fashioned molasses

1 ½ cups buttermilk

2 large eggs, slightly beaten

3 tablespoons melted butter

1 tablespoon baking powder

1 teaspoon baking soda

1 teaspoon salt

Instructions

1. Sift flour, salt, baking soda and baking powder together into a large mixing bowl. Mix in oatmeal flour to flour mixture. In a separate bowl, mix together buttermilk, eggs, melted butter and molasses, blending well, but not over-mixing. Add a little more buttermilk if too thick.
2. Add wet ingredients to flour mixture, mixing together until just combined. Do not over mix.
3. Cook on an oiled hot griddle. Keep warm in oven until ready to serve. Serve with peach or maple syrup.

TIP *To make oatmeal flour, add oatmeal to coffee grinder or Vitamix blender and grind oatmeal to a coarse flour consistency. Add to recipe.

FLORAL ESSENCE STRAWBERRY MUFFINS

Serves 4-6

One of the absolute best things about spring is the abundance of juicy, sweet strawberries. From salads to desserts, to eating them fresh or– my favorite–baking them up in a batch of mouth-watering muffins for breakfast. If you have kids, these are great as an afternoon snack with a wedge of cheddar cheese.

Ingredients

3 cups all-purpose flour

1 tablespoon baking powder

1 teaspoon baking soda

1 teaspoon fine sea salt

$1/2$ teaspoon rose water

More Ingredients

1 cup whole milk

$\frac{1}{4}$ cup heavy whipping cream

2 eggs, slightly beaten

2 sticks unsalted butter, melted

2 cups diced fresh strawberries

1 $\frac{1}{4}$ cup organic sugar

Instructions

1. Preheat oven to 350-degrees. Line muffin tins with cupcake liners or parchment paper. Sift together dry ingredients in a large mixing bowl
2. Combine eggs, milk, cream and melted butter together and mix until well-combined. Make a well in the center of the flour and pour wet ingredients into well. Add strawberries and sugar and mix until just combined. Spoon batter into lined tin filling each ¾ full.
3. Place in oven and bake until done. Muffins are done when they are browned on top and a toothpick inserted in the middle comes out clean.
4. Yield 12 muffins

SPICY SHRIMP

WITH PARMESAN GRITS

Serves 4-6

It has been said that real southerners eat grits! And if you really want to show off your southern heritage, add a nice serving of spicy shrimp over parmesan grits. I have created several recipes of this southern classic but this one is by far the absolute favorite among my family and friends.

When making this recipe, I recall while growing up the fresh catch during the summer when shrimp was netted and brought home to grace our kitchen table. These days, you can find my brother Thad on the water carrying on the tradition that began generations ago. I look forward to my summer visits and the care packages of seafood that he always has for me to bring back home to stock my freezer.

Ingredients

1 lb. large shrimp, peeled and deveined

4 cloves garlic, finely chopped

2 teaspoons shallots, finely chopped

1 jalapeno pepper, seeded and chopped

2 tablespoons tomato paste

$\frac{1}{2}$ cup coconut milk

2 tablespoons solid coconut cream

Olive oil

$\frac{1}{4}$ cup port wine

2 tablespoons fresh basil, chopped

1 teaspoon fresh thyme, minced

Kosher salt

Fresh coarse ground black pepper

Instructions

1. Peel and devein shrimp. Add to a glass bowl. Add approximately 2 tablespoons olive oil, minced garlic, and marinate for at least one half hour. Season with a little sea salt and coarse ground black pepper. Heat a cast iron skillet until hot. Add shrimp to the skillet. Brown slightly on each side for 3-5 minutes. Remove and set aside.
2. Add olive oil to the pan, enough to generously coat the bottom of the pan. Add shallots. Sauté for 1 minute. Add garlic and sauté for an additional minute, stirring constantly being careful not to burn.
3. Add tomato paste and stir until slightly browned. Be careful not to burn. Add jalapeño peppers. Add basil, thyme, black pepper and salt. Stir to combine. Add coconut milk and coconut cream. To this add ¼ cup port wine. Simmer 1-2 minutes to finish. Add grilled shrimp to sauce and heat through 3-5 minutes. Serve over parmesan grits.

PARMESAN GRITS

Ingredients

1 cup old-fashioned coarse grits (Carolina grits if available)

2 ½ cups cold water

½ cup freshly grated parmesan cheese

Instructions

1. Pour grits into a medium heavy duty pot. Add cold water from tap and rinse grits until all debris is removed. Add 2 ½ cups cold water. Cook grits over a low heat, stirring every few minutes to prevent lumps for 20-25 minutes. Add more water if necessary. Once done, add parmesan cheese and stir until completely combined.

BABY SPINACH SAUTÉ

WITH FRESH GARLIC

Serves 6

Each growing season, I look forward to harvesting the tender leaves of baby spinach from the garden. The flavor of just-picked spinach is the perfect complement to shrimp 'n grits.

Ingredients

10-12 cups fresh baby spinach

1 large bulb fresh garlic

2 tablespoons olive oil

Kosher salt, to taste

Coarse ground black pepper

Fresh lemon juice

Instructions

1. Heat a large sauce pan. Saute. Slice garlic into paper thin slivers. Add olive oil to pan. Saute garlic in oil for 1 minute. Add spinach and cover with a lid to steam for 2 minutes. Remove lid. Add salt and pepper. Toss to incorporate. Finish with a squeeze of fresh lemon juice.

"When summer is brow low and trickles down my nose, I blink once for a kind breeze and again, for the cool lull of your hand in mine." -Dorhora

SUMMER BREEZE

When I think of my southern roots the imagery is almost always that of the wind blowing through mossy trees, moving the air just enough to stir up sudden cloud bursts to usher in a cool southern breeze. I love the smells of summer along with the squeals of laughter that permeate the air as children momentarily toss aside the cares of being dutiful and busy themselves with play. Ahhh, summer breezes and children at play - the perfect recipe for a good summer day.

Grilled Jerk Pork Tenderloin
Mango Pepper Chutney
Shaved Beet Salad with Avocado & Goat Cheese
Chicken Florentine Quiche
Hot Crab Dip with with Fresh Herb Crackers
Eggplant Panini with Tapenade
Roasted Vegetable Lasagna
Fried Green Tomatoes with Spicy Mayonnaise
Grilled Herbed Steak with Cabbage Slaw
Peach Bacon Bites
Southern Fried Oysters with Remoulade Sauce
Grilled Jerk Fish with Peach Chutney
Grilled Salmon with Chili Peppers
Seared Scallops with Mixed Greens
Mussels on the Grill
Salmon with Dill, Lemon, & Garlic Butter
White Bean Soup with Pesto
Kale Salad
Whole Bream with Roasted Fennel
Mediterranean Summer Salad
Thai Basil Fried Rice with Sausage

GRILLED JERK PORK TENDERLOIN

Serves 8-10

Where I grew up, in Central Florida, the influence of Jamaican cuisine is very prevalent. From curry goat to jerk pork and chicken, the cultures of African American and the rich island of Jamaica are very well blended. During the summer months, it is not uncommon to find most cookouts and barbecues with jerk on the menu.

This recipe is at its best when you allow the pork to marinate for at least 24 hours before popping it onto a hot grill. Serve up with a nice fresh mango chutney for a dish your family and friends will remember for years to come.

Ingredients

1 4-5 lb. pork tenderloin

3-5 teaspoons medium or hot jerk seasonings (Walkerswood is a very good brand)

6 cloves garlic, slivered

Olive oil

Instructions

1. Place tenderloin on a large glass rectangular dish. Cut tiny slits in areas of the meat. Insert garlic cloves in each slit. Combine olive oil and jerk seasonings in a small bowl. Rub the seasoning onto the tenderloin, making sure to cover the entire loin. Be sure to rub the seasoning into the slits as well. Cover the tenderloin with plastic wrap and marinate overnight or for at least 2 hours.

2. Heat up a gas or charcoal grill. Place tenderloin onto grill and cook on a low to medium setting with the top down. Check tenderloin occasionally to make sure not to burn. Grill until done or until a meat thermometer reaches 145 -160 degrees, when inserted into the center of the loin. When done, remove from grill, wrap in aluminum foil, and allow to rest for at least 3 minutes before serving. This will allow the juices to flow throughout the meat. Slice into 2 inch slices and serve up with a side of mango chutney.

3. This dish can also be roasted in the oven. To roast, preheat the oven to 425 degrees. Place pork on a pan with a rack and roast for 15 minutes. Reduce oven to 325 degrees and continue baking until thermometer reaches 145-160 degrees. Remove from the oven and allow to rest before serving.

MANGO PEPPER CHUTNEY

I love special deliveries and my southern family never disappoint me. Each year, like clockwork, I can count on a package of sweet, fragrant mangoes from my Florida family. And since you can only eat so many mangoes and since I don't want to risk them going bad, I pull out the canning jars and make a big batch of chutney.

This recipe is especially good with jerk pork tenderloin, but my favorite is with jerk fish.

Ingredients

1 cup white vinegar

2 cups sugar

6 cups chopped fresh mango

1 yellow onion, chopped

1 teaspoon minced ginger

1 clove garlic, minced

¾ cups golden raisins

1 teaspoon brown mustard seeds

½ teaspoon red pepper flakes

Instructions

1. Add sugar and vinegar to a heavy duty saucepan and stir to combine. Place on a medium flame and bring to a boil. Add remaining ingredients to vinegar mixture and simmer for 45-50 minutes until mixture becomes thick and syrupy.
2. Add to hot sterilized jars. Tighten lids until just closed, but not overly tight. Place chutney in a canning bath and simmer for 10 minutes. Remove from bath and tighten completely. Invert jars on a rack to cool and to force air from the jars. When cool, test the seal by pressing the lid. If it pops, repeat the bath process. Store in a cool place until ready to use.

SHAVED BEET SALAD

WITH AVOCADO &
GOAT CHEESE

Serves 4-6

Light, refreshing and oh so good on a hot summer day! Enough said!

Ingredients

3-4 fresh beets (red and gold)

1 large avocado

3 oz. goat cheese

Kosher salt and coarse ground black pepper, to taste

Lemon balsamic vinegar reduction

Instructions

1. Scrub beets until clean. Place beets in aluminum foil, seal and roast in 350-degree oven until just tender. Remove from oven and cool completely. Using a very sharp knife, julienne beets and place in a medium size glass or metal bowl.
2. Peel and remove pit from avocado. Cut into medium chunks and add to beets. Toss gently. Spoon onto salad plates, dividing into 4 servings. Add salt and pepper and crumbled goat cheese. Drizzle with lavender balsamic vinegar reduction. To reduce balsamic vinegar add 3-4 tablespoons to a small saucepan and simmer until vinegar thickens. Cool.

CHICKEN FLORENTINE QUICHE

Serves 8-10

If you want to impress your guests, let them eat quiche! But make sure, it is full of flavor and baked up in a good flaky crust! I am an advocate for eating and serving up real food and to keep it healthy; I believe in eating what you love, but in moderation.

This recipe is filled with all kinds of wonderful ingredients, making for one of the best dishes you can ever put on a plate.

This was the most popular dish at my bakery & cafe and on occasion I will happen upon a former guest of the bakery who shares how much they miss this special treat.

Ingredients

Signature Pie Crust

3 grilled herbed chicken breasts, cut into small chunks

1 cup steamed, chopped spinach & baby kale

$1/8$ cup finely chopped sun-dried tomatoes

$1/4$ cup feta cheese

Dried herbs (basil, thyme, dried oregano and granulated garlic)

Kosher salt and fresh ground black pepper

$1/2$ chopped onion, sauté in 1 tablespoon olive oil

3 cloves chopped garlic

Base Ingredients

8 eggs

2 cups heavy whipping cream

2 cups whole milk

$\frac{1}{2}$ teaspoon kosher salt

1 teaspoon fresh ground black pepper

$\frac{1}{2}$ teaspoon cayenne pepper

$\frac{1}{2}$ teaspoon nutmeg

Instructions

1. Begin by rolling out pie crust and placing in a spring form baking pan. Place crust in freezer and chill until firm. In the meantime, preheat oven to 350 degrees. When firm, remove crust from freezer and line crust with parchment paper and fill with dried beans. Blind-bake in oven until edges begin to turn light brown. Remove beans and parchment paper and return pie crust to oven and bake until done.
2. Wrap pan with aluminum foil. This will catch any possible spills. Layer chicken and other filler ingredients, beginning with chicken, continuing until all has been put into pan.
3. In a large mixing bowl, lightly beat together base ingredients and slowly pour egg mixture over ingredients in pie crust. Return quiche to oven and bake until done; about 45-50 minutes. Quiche is done when a skewer or slender knife inserted in center comes out clean. Remove from oven and allow to rest for 10-15 minutes before cutting.

HOT CRAB DIP

WITH FRESH HERB CRACKERS

Serves 8-10

This recipe for hot crab dip goes so well with homemade crackers. And if you really want to spice it up, add a dash of good hot pepper sauce.

Ingredients

1 lb. lump crab meat

8 oz. cream cheese, softened

½ cup freshly grated parmesan cheese

¾ cup Duke's or your favorite mayonnaise

2 tablespoons minced yellow onion

1 teaspoon horseradish

1 teaspoon Worcestershire sauce

½ teaspoon kosher salt

2 tablespoons hot pepper sauce

Instructions

1. Preheat oven to 325 degrees. Butter a one quart baking dish. Blend all ingredients in a food processor except parmesan cheese until smooth. Pour into baking dish. Top with parmesan cheese. Bake until hot and bubbly. Remove and serve with fresh homemade crackers.

FRESH HERB CRACKERS

Growing up, one of the most used phrases around my grandparents' home was, "waste not, want not." Having learned this lesson, I always find ways to repurpose ingredients when making recipes.

This fresh cracker is made using leftover pie crust dough or if you want to just make up a batch for your next party, that works too.

These crackers are as simple to make as can be and they also store well when placed in a jar with a tight seal. Don't be afraid to try your own favorite spices for a different twist on this delectable recipe.

Ingredients

Recipe for 1 pie crust or leftover pie dough

Fresh grated parmesan cheese

Dried fresh herb medley (thyme, basil, oregano)

Instructions

1. Roll out chilled pie crust on a lightly-floured surface. Sprinkle herbs and parmesan cheese evenly over the entire pie crust. Roll herbs and cheese into crust using rolling pin. Cut cracker rounds using a cookie cutter. Place rounds onto cookie sheet. Bake in pre-heated 350 degree oven until lightly browned around the edges. Remove crackers from cookie sheet and cool on a metal cooling rack. Serve with your favorite dips or mild cheeses. This is also scrumptious as a topping for soups.

EGGPLANT PANINI

WITH TAPENADE

Serves 6-8

This is the absolute best recipe for the first harvest of eggplant from the garden. The flavor of homegrown eggplant is unmatched by what you might find at the market. For the best flavor, pick before they become too large. If you are choosing from the market, be sure to pass on eggplant with dry or soft spots as this is a telltale sign that they have been in the market too long, which means they have lost most of their good flavor.

This sandwich was one of the favorites of our guests at my former bakery and cafe. The recipe can be made ahead of time, assembled and grilled right before serving.

Ingredients

2 large eggplants, sliced crosswise

Olive oil

Red wine vinegar

Dried herbs (thyme, basil, oregano)

1 teaspoon kosher salt

1 tablespoon fresh ground coarse black pepper

6 slices Swiss cheese

Focaccia bread

Instructions

1. Add sliced eggplant to a glass bowl. Add olive oil, red wine vinegar, herbs, salt and pepper. Cover with plastic wrap.
2. Slice Focaccia into 6 inch squares. Slice through center to create a pocket for the sandwich. Layer one side of the bread slices with eggplant slices and tapenade (recipe follows). Add 1 slice Swiss cheese. Close the sandwich with the other half of bread. Press together. Brush with a little olive oil and add to heated panini griddle. Cook until brown and cheese is bubbling.

TAPENADE

Ingredients

1 cup Kalamata olives

2 cloves fresh garlic, crushed

2 tablespoons olive oil

2 tablespoons red wine vinegar

1 teaspoon fresh lemon juice

1 teaspoon organic sugar

1 teaspoon fresh ground black pepper

Instructions

1. Drain olives. Peel and crush garlic. Place olives and garlic in small food processor. Add oil, vinegar, lemon juice, sugar and black pepper. Process until smooth.

ROASTED VEGETABLE LASAGNA

Serves 6-8

At the peak of the summer harvest, the garden is lush with all kinds of wonderful vegetables and this recipe makes good use of some of the best of the crop. This can be made ahead of time and baked just before serving for a stress-free dinnertime.

Ingredients

4-6 small yellow squash, sliced lengthwise

4-6 zucchini squash, sliced lengthwise

6 medium carrots, thinly sliced lengthwise

1 large yellow onion, thinly sliced

1 medium red onion, thinly sliced

1 large parsnip, thinly sliced lengthwise

12 large roasted garlic cloves

¼ lb. smoked provolone cheese

4 oz. shredded mozzarella cheese

¼ cup freshly grated parmesan cheese

8 oz. ricotta cheese

2 tablespoons fresh rosemary, finely chopped

1 teaspoon kosher salt

½ teaspoon ground nutmeg

1 teaspoon coarse ground black pepper

Instructions

1. Add vegetables to a large bowl and toss with a generous amount of olive oil. Spread vegetables in single layer onto cookie sheets and place in a 375-degree oven. Roast vegetables until tender and slightly crusted around the edges. Remove from oven. You can also roast vegetables on the outside grill.

2. Oil a 9x13 baking dish. In a small bowl mix together, ricotta cheese, rosemary, salt, pepper, and nutmeg.

3. Add a layer of vegetables to the bottom of the baking dish. Top with spoonfuls of ricotta cheese. Continue layering vegetables and ricotta cheese mixture until complete ending with a layer of vegetables. Top with mozzarella, provolone, and parmesan cheeses.

4. Loosely cover with aluminum foil, making sure to leave room for steam to escape. Bake in a preheated 350-degree oven or outside grill that has a cover, until bubbly. Remove foil and continue baking for another 5-8 minutes until slightly browned.

FRIED GREEN TOMATOES

WITH SPICY MAYONNAISE

Serves 4-6

Although I am not a huge fan of fried foods, especially when it comes to vegetables, fried green tomatoes is something I cannot resist. Each year I look forward to the first harvest from the garden of slightly under ripe tomatoes to slice and season for this special treat. Fried green tomatoes, when done right, should be crispy on the outside, not greasy, and tender on the inside. This recipe meets all those requirements and I am almost certain that once you make up a batch, you will wholeheartedly agree.

Ingredients

2 large green beefsteak tomatoes, sliced

Kosher salt

1 cup all-purpose flour

1 tablespoon Cajun seasoning

½ cup buttermilk

1 egg, lightly beaten

⅓ cup cornmeal

½ cup fine dry bread crumbs

¼ cup peanut or avocado oil

Instructions

1. Mix together the flour, salt, and Cajun seasoning in a small bowl. In a larger bowl beat egg and milk, until blended. Mix together bread crumbs and cornmeal in separate shallow bowl. Heat oil in a large skillet. Dip tomato slices in flour, then egg mixture, and finally in the bread crumb mixture. Fry 3- 5 minutes on each side and drain. Serve with spicy mayonnaise. (Recipe follows)

SPICY MAYONNAISE

Ingredients

1 cup mayonnaise

2 tablespoon hot sauce

¼ teaspoon granulated garlic

Instructions

1. Mix mayonnaise, hot sauce and garlic. Serve as a condiment with fried green tomatoes.

GRILLED HERBED STEAK

WITH CABBAGE SLAW

Serves 4-6

For years, flank steak was considered a cheaper cut of beef; that is until chefs, yours truly included, discovered how versatile and scrumptious this very fine cut of beef could be. This recipe is big on flavor and the longer you marinate, the bigger the flavor. This recipe is also great on salads and served on a crusty sandwich bread, such as ciabatta with caramelized onions and bleu cheese.

Ingredients

2-3 lb. flank steak

1 tablespoon each, basil, thyme, oregano

1 teaspoon coarse black pepper

1 tablespoon granulated garlic

1 tablespoon kosher salt

2 tablespoons fresh rosemary, finely chopped

2 cloves fresh garlic, thinly sliced

2 tablespoons olive oil

½ cup good dry red wine

Instructions

1. Place steak onto a cutting board. Using a very sharp knife, cut surface slits on one side of the steak. Insert garlic slivers into slits. In a small bowl, combine herbs, granulated garlic, salt and rosemary. Rub steak with the mixture, making sure to rub into slits. Put seasoned steak into a large zip lock bag. Pour olive oil and wine over steak. Seal bag. Rotate bag to distribute wine and olive oil. Marinate for at least 3 hours.
2. Preheat grill. Grill steak on hot grill until seared to a light crust on each side but still a little pink in the thickest part of the meat. Remove from grill and let rest on cutting board for a few minutes. Slice steak into thin slices cutting across the grain. Serve over a bed of red cabbage slaw. (Recipe follows)

CABBAGE SLAW

Ingredients

1 small red cabbage, shredded

2 tablespoons minced red onion

2 julienned Granny Smith apples

1 teaspoon celery seeds

1 tablespoon cream honey

Dressing

¾ cup Duke's light mayonnaise

4 tablespoons red wine vinegar

4 teaspoons organic sugar

Dash granulated garlic

1 tablespoon olive oil

1 teaspoon lemon juice

Instructions

1. Add cabbage, onion, apples, celery seed and honey to a large bowl. In a separate bowl, mix together ingredients for dressing. Pour dressing over cabbage mixture and toss to combine.

PEACH BACON BITES

If you love entertaining friends and family during the summer months, then prepare yourself to make quite an impression with this luscious grilled peach recipe. Be sure to choose peaches that are ripe, but somewhat firm to make sure they hold together when grilled. You are going to love the melding together of the flavors of tartness from the cheese, saltiness from the bacon and sweetness from the peaches. Be sure to make extra, because, like peanuts and chips, one serving will not be enough.

Ingredients

12 Strips bacon cut in half crosswise (Turkey bacon is a good alternative)

6 ripe, firm, fresh peaches, peeled, pitted

6 slices Swiss cheese, cut into 2-inch strips

6 teaspoons packed brown sugar

1 teaspoon cinnamon

1 teaspoon chili powder

$\frac{1}{2}$ teaspoon cayenne pepper

Instructions

1. Cook bacon in skillet, medium heat until just brown but a little limp. Place on plate covered with paper towels to drain excess fat.
2. Wrap a slice of cheese around each peach slice and on top of this wrap with bacon. Secure with a wooden toothpick.
3. In small bowl, blend remaining ingredients. Dip both sides of each bacon bite in sugar pressing into bacon to coat completely. Place each onto an oiled cookie sheet. Broil 4 inches from heat 2 – 3 minutes.

SOUTHERN FRIED OYSTERS

WITH REMOULADE SAUCE

Serves 4-6

Ingredients

16 oz. fresh oysters

2 large eggs, slightly beaten

¾ cup all-purpose flour

1 teaspoon salt

1 teaspoon fresh ground black pepper

1 teaspoon granulated garlic

1 cup corn meal

½ cup milk

1 tablespoon olive or vegetable oil

1 lemon

Vegetable oil for frying

Instructions

1. Arrange 3 large plates to assemble ingredients. Add flour, salt, black pepper and granulated garlic in first plate and whisk together. In second plate add eggs, olive oil and milk and blend well. In third plate, add corn meal.
2. Heat oil in a cast iron skillet, enough to come half way up sides of skillet. Dredge oysters first in flour mixture, then in egg and lastly in corn meal. Add in single pieces the coated oysters to the hot oil. Cook on one side until brown and then turn to complete frying. Remove from skillet and drain on platter that has been lined with paper towels to remove excess oil.
3. Once drained, transfer oysters to a clean platter and drizzle with fresh lemon juice. Serve with hot pepper sauce and remoulade sauce (recipe follows).

REMOULADE SAUCE

Ingredients

1 cup mayonnaise

1 tablespoon white vinegar

1 tablespoon pure honey

1 tablespoon tomato paste

1 teaspoon fresh garlic, finely minced

1 teaspoon onion, finely chopped

1 tablespoon strong yellow mustard

1 teaspoon horseradish

1 tablespoon fresh lemon juice

Instructions

1. Add all ingredients to a small mixing bowl and mix to combine completely. Store in refrigerator until ready to serve.

GRILLED JERK FISH

WITH PEACH CHUTNEY

Serves 4-6

During the summer months, the last thing you want to do is stand over a hot stove. Fish is a great mainstay during the summer season and is typically very popular because it does not weigh you down and it only takes a few minutes to prepare.

I also like to take advantage of the availability of fresh fruit to create delicious side dishes to top things off. For this recipe, I usually serve up a blanket of my peach chutney. Overall, this dish is easy, healthy and the taste is absolutely divine.

Ingredients

4 medium trout or other firm fish, scaled and cleaned

2-4 teaspoons Grace Jerk or Walkerswood Jerk Seasoning, medium hot

Granulated garlic

2 tablespoons Olive oil

Instructions

1. Mix together olive oil, granulated garlic and "Grace" brand Jamaican jerk seasoning in a small bowl until well-blended. Cut 2 horizontal slits (at an angle) on both sides of each fish.
2. Lay fish on a cookie sheet and with your fingers rub jerk mixture on both sides making sure to put a little seasoning in slits to increase flavor. You will only need a thin coating on each fish. Be sure to keep the jerk seasoning light as it is very spicy. Cover cookie sheet and fish entirely with plastic wrap and refrigerate for at least one hour or overnight.
3. Heat grill until very hot. Spray the surface of two metal cookie cooling racks with cooking spray or coat the racks with a grill brush that has been dipped in olive oil. Place one rack on top of grill grate. Place each fish onto grill surface leaving space between each; lower the flame. Place second rack on top of fish. Close cover and grill on one side until brown and crispy.
4. Using two long metal tongs, flip racks to cook fish on other side. Grill fish until brown and crispy. Be sure to monitor to prevent burning. Fish is done when tested with a fork and it flakes easily. Remove fish from grill and place on serving platter. Add peach chutney to the platter and serve. (recipe follows)

PEACH CHUTNEY

Ingredients

1 dozen fresh ripe white or yellow peaches, peeled, sliced, and cut into 1" pieces*

½ diced red onion

Spice bouquet** (cinnamon stick-broken into 2" pieces, cloves, nutmeg)

1 teaspoon each — mace, tarragon, grated fresh ginger, allspice

1 clove minced garlic

½ teaspoon sea or Kosher salt

Lemon zest and juice from 1 lemon

¼ c. apple cider vinegar

¼ cup apple cider

1 cup brown sugar

garlic

Instructions

1. Add peaches and red onion to a medium size glass bowl. Toss with 1 teaspoon lemon juice to prevent fruit from turning brown. Set aside. Add sugar, salt, lemon juice & zest, ginger, apple cider vinegar and apple cider to a small pot.

2. Place on stove and bring to a simmer (most grills have cooking eyes so this can be prepared outdoors). Add spice bouquet, cover and simmer until mixture develops a syrup and mixture lightly coats a metal spoon.

3. Pour mixture and spice bouquet over peaches. Cool. Cover bowl with plastic wrap and allow to rest for at least two hours for maximum flavor.

TIP *White peaches are a great option for this recipe; they are very fragrant with a distinct floral essence. I prefer them over the yellow although the yellow peaches are also quite good.

**For spice bouquet please use whole spices.

GRILLED SALMON

WITH CHILI PEPPERS

Serves 4

This recipe is so easy and amazingly good! The ingredients are simple and during the warmer months, it is the perfect opportunity to take advantage of fresh thyme and salad greens. Preparation time is less than 30 minutes, leaving just enough time to spend outdoors planting that vegetable garden.

Ingredients

2 red chili peppers, seeded and finely chopped

2 jalapeno peppers, seeded and chopped

1 tablespoon chopped chipotle in adobo

½ finely chopped onion

3 cloves garlic, chopped

½ cup chopped cilantro

1 teaspoon ground cumin

¼ cup fresh-squeezed lime juice

¼ cup olive oil

1 teaspoon kosher salt

1 salmon filet cut into four pieces

Grilling planks

Instructions

1. Combine all ingredients, minus salmon, in a small glass bowl to make marinade. Place salmon onto a baking sheet or large plate. Top salmon with marinade mixture, dividing it equally between the four pieces. Cover with plastic wrap, place in refrigerator and allow to marinate for 10-15 minutes.
2. Remove from refrigerator and place on wooden cooking planks that have been prepared according to manufacturer's instructions. Place on grill and close cover or bake in a 375-degree oven until done, about 15 minutes.
3. Be careful not to overcook. The fish is done when it flakes easily when pricked with a fork and is a little undercooked in the center. Fish will continue to cook when removed from the grill and result in a dish that is cooked to perfection.

SEARED SCALLOPS

WITH MIXED GREENS

Serves 4-6

Springtime is one of my favorite times of the year, perfect for harvesting the first of the cool weather salad greens. I especially love this recipe because not only is it delicious, but it is also a great way to keep the calories in check as you work to get ready for swimsuit weather.

Ingredients

1 lb. Sea Scallops

Garlic infused olive oil

Kosher Salt

Fresh Ground Black Pepper

Instructions

1. Preheat oven to 375-degrees. Prepare scallops by making sure they are free of sand. If sandy, use a wet paper towel to clean. Heat 2 tablespoons olive oil in a hot oven-proof saute pan. Add 2 cloves fresh garlic. Simmer in oil for about 2 minutes, being careful not to burn.
2. Remove garlic from oil and remove half of oil from pan. Add scallops and sear on one side. Do not overcook. Turn scallops and transfer pan to oven. Bake for no longer than 2 minutes. Remove pan from oven.
3. Add to individual plates that have been prepared with fresh mesclun salad greens. Finish with salt and pepper.
4. You can also add balsamic vinegar to pan once scallops have been removed. To make balsamic vinegar dressing, add 4 tablespoons balsamic vinegar to sauce pan. Reduce heat and simmer until the sauce thickens just a bit. Pour over prepared scallops and greens. Serve immediately.

MUSSELS ON THE GRILL

Serves 4-6

Although I dream about cold nights in front of a crackling fire, truth be told, I am really a warm weather kind of girl. Warm weather means not only do I get to play in the dirt in the garden, but I also get to move my kitchen outdoors.

This recipe for grilled mussels is best if you use a gas grill, although a charcoal grill can also work if you have one that can be covered. Another technique if using a charcoal grill is to use an aluminum pan to cover the mussels or create a tent using heavy-duty aluminum foil. The idea is to capture as much heat as possible to create that amazing sizzle.

Ingredients

2 lbs. fresh or frozen mussels on the half shell

3 tablespoons melted butter

2 tablespoons olive oil

6 cloves fresh garlic, chopped

4 tablespoons fresh herbs consisting of parsley, basil and oregano

Fresh lemons

¾ tablespoons kosher salt

1 teaspoon coarse black pepper

6 tablespoons freshly grated parmesan cheese

Instructions

1. Heat up grill. Arrange mussels on a foil lined cookie sheet. Add herbs, garlic, salt and pepper to a small food processor. Blend until coarsely ground.
2. Transfer herb mixture to a small glass bowl. Add olive oil and butter to herbs. Stir in parmesan cheese.

Instructions Continued

3.   Spoon mixture on top of mussels, dividing evenly. Drizzle olive oil over tops of mussels. Add pan to grill and lower cover. Cook for about 10 minutes. Remove pan from the grill.

4.   Serve with fresh lemons.

SALMON

WITH DILL, LEMON, & GARLIC BUTTER

Serves 6-8

This recipe can be served hot or cold and makes for a nice presentation for elegant buffets or for family-style dinners.

To serve cold, accompany with chopped red onions, boiled eggs, horseradish, and grainy brown mustard.

Ingredients

1 wild-caught or farm-raised organic salmon filet

2 tablespoons olive oil

1 tablespoon unsalted butter

2 teaspoons fresh dill

2 large garlic cloves cut into very thin slivers

Juice of one large lemon

½ fresh lime

Kosher salt and coarse ground black pepper, to taste

Instructions

1. Heat oven to 375 degrees. Place salmon on a large, oiled cookie sheet or baking pan. In a small sauce pan, melt butter. Add olive oil to butter. Add remaining ingredients and heat through.
2. Coat salmon with butter mixture. Place in oven and bake until fish has just a hint of pink in very center. Remove from oven and allow to rest. Finish with a squeeze of fresh lime juice.

TIP Fish will continue to cook once removed from oven so be careful not to overcook.

WHITE BEAN SOUP

WITH PESTO

Serves 6-8

White bean soup, or what southerners call navy beans, brings back fond memories of growing up in the south. This is a healthier version of what I grew up eating, which was usually cooked with pork hocks. Topped with fresh pesto, I promise you will not be deprived of flavor.

This soup is low on cost, high in protein and low in calories. Definitely fits the category of "good choices" for you and your family!

Ingredients

1 small bag navy beans

1 large yellow onion, chopped

3 cloves garlic, chopped

Kosher salt

Fresh ground black pepper

Basil pesto (store-bought or see recipe below)

Smoked Turkey (optional)

Olive oil, about 4 tbs.

Instructions

1. Spread beans onto a cookie sheet and examine, removing any pebbles and dirt. Transfer beans to a large glass bowl, add water and rinse thoroughly. Add enough water to bowl to cover beans entirely plus about 6 inches of additional water as beans will expand once soaked; cover with plastic wrap. Place in the refrigerator and soak overnight. For a quick soak, put beans in a large pot, cover with water and bring to a boil. Lower heat and simmer for about 5 minutes. Turn off heat and allow to soak for one hour.
2. To prepare recipe, add olive oil to a hot large heavy-duty pot. Sauté onions until translucent, or about 3 minutes. Add garlic and sauté an additional 2 minutes. If using smoked turkey, add turkey pieces and stir. Do not add salt if using smoked turkey or reduce the amount of salt to prevent over-salting. Cover pot with a lid, reduce heat to low and allow turkey to "sweat" for about 3 minutes.

3. Add soaked beans and about 5 cups of water. Add salt and pepper. Bring to a boil, reduce heat and cook beans until tender. When finished cooking, remove half of the beans (not turkey), and put into a food processor or blender. Puree beans until smooth. Return to pot and stir completely.

4. To serve, spoon into your favorite bowl and top with 1 tablespoon basil pesto and or a little chili oil for an extra kick. Enjoy!

TIP Pesto is made using pine nuts, so if you have someone who is sensitive or allergic to nuts, do not use.

PESTO

Ingredients

1 ½ cups fresh basil leaves

2 cloves garlic

¼ cup pine nuts

¾ cup Parmesan Cheese

¼ cup olive oil

Instructions

1. Place all ingredients into a food processor and process until well-blended or the consistency is smooth like butter. Remove from food processor and store in glass canning jar in the refrigerator until ready to use.

KALE SALAD

This amazing superfood is at its best when eaten raw. And there is no better way to dress it up than to create a salad filled with wonderful additions to make your taste buds burst with delight.

For lunch you can load it up with other vegetables like avocado, shaved brussel sprouts and cucumber. And to make it even more robust and flavorful, add things like pomegranate, apple, grapes, and toasted nuts. Being a true southern girl, pecans are my favorite.

When in the mood for a satisfying dinner salad, the addition of grilled chicken or salmon makes this hearty salad just right.

Ingredients

1 bunch of kale leaves

1 small navel orange, peeled and seeded

½ cup seedless raisins, white or dark

½ cup chopped toasted pecans or walnuts

2-3 carrots, julienned or roughly shredded

1 cup seedless grapes sliced in half

1 cup fresh blueberries

1 Honey Crisp apple, peeled cored and cut into chunks

2 tablespoons extra-virgin olive oil

1 tablespoons red wine vinegar

¼ – ½ of an onion or one stalk green onion/scallion, optional

Kosher salt and fresh ground black pepper, to taste

Instructions

1. Rinse kale and chop into small pieces. Peel, seed, and dice apple into small chunks. Peel and shred carrots. Cut grapes in half or quarters. Peel orange and remove seeds. Cut orange into small sections. If using onion, chop into small pieces.
2. Combine the kale and remaining fruit in a large salad bowl. In a small bowl, combine olive oil, red wine vinegar, and salt and pepper and 1 teaspoon raw honey. Whisk together. Pour over the salad and toss. Sprinkle nuts on top and toss once again.

WHOLE BREAM

WITH ROASTED FENNEL

Serves 4-6

One of my favorite fish, even to this day, is fresh water bream. Growing up in the South, this was by far a favorite of my family. Bream is a sweet fish with a light flavor, which means you can add all kinds of wonderful flavors without running the risk of having them clash with the main attraction. Since moving away, I have found great substitutes for the familiar flavor in other varieties such as porgies, rock, or sea trout. The addition of fennel gives this dish a very unique flavor.

Ingredients

2 large bream or rock fish

1 large bulb fennel

Kosher Salt

Fresh Coarse Ground Black Pepper

Olive oil

Instructions

1. Have your fish market clean a 2-3 lb. fish by scaling and removing insides of fish. I typically have them remove the backbone of the fish as well. To prepare, cut diagonal lines across body of fish on both sides.
2. Rinse fennel and pat dry with a paper towel until dry. Remove outer portion of fennel bulb and cut away top portion and set aside. Cut fennel through the middle and then slice into 1 inch sections.
3. Lightly coat a skillet with olive oil. Season fish with salt and pepper to taste. Remove the sprigs from top of fennel bulb and layer the sprigs inside the fish. Coat fish with a little olive oil and place onto baking dish.
4. Layer additional sprigs of fennel on top of fish and coat with a little more olive oil. Add bulb pieces on baking dish around fish and season with salt and pepper to taste. Drizzle with a little olive oil and toss to coat.

5. Bake in a very hot oven — 425-450 degrees for about 12 minutes. Reduce heat to 375 degrees and continue baking for an additional 10-15 minutes. Fish should be crispy when done, but not overcooked. To test for doneness, using a fork, insert into thickest part of fish and if it flakes or separates, it is done.

TIP Be sure to turn the fennel as it starts to brown around the edges. Serve fish and fennel with fingerling potatoes or rice and sautéed green beans or your favorite green vegetable.

MEDITERRANEAN SUMMER SALAD

Serves 6-8

Warm weather calls for meals that are hearty but lite and chocked full of fresh vegetables and herbs that are so plentiful during the warmer months.

Here is a variation of a Salad Nicoise that uses pasta as a substitute for red potatoes.

Ingredients

3 cups cooked dried pasta

Blanched fresh green beans

6 oz. water-packed tuna or grilled fresh tuna, if available

2 large ripe avocados, cut into chunks

6-8 grape tomatoes or 3 large plum tomatoes, cut into halves

3 hard-boiled eggs, shelled and sliced

Small bunch of fresh basil leaves

2-3 oz. anchovy fillets, drained

Black and Kalamata Olives

Capers, to taste

Dressing

¼ cup extra virgin olive oil

2 large cloves garlic, crushed

2 tablespoons red wine vinegar

½ teaspoon Dijon mustard

2 tablespoons fresh basil, chopped

Kosher salt and freshly ground black pepper, to taste

Instructions

1. For the dressing, whisk all ingredients in a medium glass or stainless steel bowl. Add salt and pepper to taste.
2. For the salad, drain pasta, blanch green beans, and trim. Slice tomatoes and begin arranging in a large shallow salad bowl.
3. Begin by arranging a bed of tomatoes on the bottom of the bowl. Drizzle a little of the salad dressing over the tomatoes and sprinkle a little salt and pepper. Add several leaves of the basil on top of the dressing and tomatoes and follow up with pasta that has been tossed with a little of the dressing.
4. Add tuna on top of this along with additional basil, avocado, green beans, and anchovies. Drizzle remainder of the dressing over the salad and garnish with basil leaves.

THAI BASIL FRIED RICE

WITH SAUSAGE

Serves 6-8

If your family loves fried rice, then this recipe is going to become one of your favorites. To make this recipe extra hearty, I add chicken sausage. There is a long list of vegetables. However, you can feel free to shorten the list if you desire. Keep in mind too that this is a great way to load up on the vegetables for kids, who tend to like this dish. It is very simple to make, very economical, and packed with good nutrition.

If you choose, you can use one of my favorite substitutes–black rice rather than the brown rice listed in the recipe. Black rice does require an extra step, however, requiring soaking before preparation. Simply follow the directions on the package. You can purchase black rice at any specialty food store or some of your higher-end supermarkets.

Ingredients

1 ½ cups brown rice (black rice is an option)

3 cups chicken or vegetable stock

Small bunch Thai Basil (available at Asian markets)

4-5 cloves garlic

1 medium yellow onion, chopped

2 scallions, chopped

2 carrots, chopped

2 zucchini squash, chopped

1 yellow squash, chopped

1 cup baby spinach, chopped

6 stalks asparagus, chopped

More Ingredients

3 Apple-Chicken sausage, sliced

soy sauce

Fresh ground black pepper

2 eggs, slightly beaten

Olive & sesame oil

Instructions

1. Add rice to a large pot along with stock and cover with a lid. Bring to a slow boil; reduce heat and simmer until completely done.
2. Remove rice from pot and spread onto a cookie sheet and allow to cool completely. Cover rice with foil or plastic wrap and place in refrigerator, preferably overnight.
3. Prepare all vegetables, by washing and chopping. In a large hot wok or heavy sauté pan, add about 4 tablespoons olive oil to pan.
4. Begin stir-fry with onions and cook until tender, tossing very fast to prevent steaming of vegetables. Add scallions and sauté about a minute. Follow with remaining vegetables, ending with garlic. Sauté in between each addition of vegetable until just tender. If necessary, add an additional tablespoon of oil to prevent sticking.
5. Remove vegetables from pan, temporarily placing on a cookie sheet. Lower heat to medium. Lightly coat pan or wok and brown sausage. Remove sausage. Raise heat and add 1 teaspoon sesame oil to pan. Add rice and sauté until completely coated with oil and very hot. Add vegetables in thirds and sauté between each addition to completely dry out any liquid from vegetable and rice mixture.
6. Add chopped basil and sauté. Add black pepper, granulated garlic and 2 tablespoons Soy sauce to mixture. Continue to toss mixing thoroughly. Scramble 2 eggs in lightly coated skillet until just set. Chop and toss into rice mixture. Add chicken sausage to mixture. Serve.

"It's the little things, the seemingly insignificant things that create moments of joy!"

LUNCHTIME FAVORITES

Midday in the south is always special as this is the time of day when you retreat and allow the sun to do what it does best; shine. It is also the time of day when things typically slow down which means you want to keep whatever you are serving up for lunch on the lite side.

Salads with very little protein are always good choices, but if you insist on meat, keep the portions small and heap on lots of the green stuff. Make use of as much of fresh vegetables and vine fruit from the garden. (You did plant that garden didn't you?) Keep in mind too, that in order to enjoy the amazing taste of fresh food, be sure to not be heavy-handed when pouring on the salad dressings.

And because all kinds of fruits and vegetables are always in abundance in warmer climates, use lunchtime as an excuse to be creative.

✺

Summer Heirloom Tomato Salad with Basil & Blueberries
Steak on Ciabatta with Caramelized Onions & Bleu Cheese
Farro with Curry & Apricots
Hearty Roasted Root Vegetable Soup
Grilled Chicken on Ciabatta with Apricot Chutney & Brie
Rustic Flatbread Pizza
Curry Lentil Stew
Avocado, Tomato, & Peach Salad
Hearty Tomato Soup with Coconut Milk
Avocado on Whole Grain Bread
Sun-Dried Tomato Basil Pesto Mayonnaise
Penne Pasta with Spicy Mushroom Medley

✺

SUMMER HEIRLOOM TOMATO SALAD

WITH BASIL AND BLUEBERRIES

Serves 4-6

Blueberries and tomatoes are a staple on the southern table. During the summer months, it is not uncommon to catch me wiping off a just plucked tomato from the vine and biting into it as my own special way of treating myself while working in the garden. Tomatoes are at their tastiest-best when picked right from the vine. Their natural sweetness is enough to satisfy even the pickiest of eaters. When my children were little you could always find them wandering through the garden grabbing handfuls of cherry tomatoes and popping them into their little mouths. And since I do not use chemicals, the joy of eating from the vine was never interrupted.

The combination of tomatoes, blueberries and basil in this recipe will make your taste buds sing with delight. A light drizzle of vinaigrette, and you are in heaven. Nice as a side dish for chicken or fish or as a light lunch. A small wedge of cheddar cheese or smoked Gouda is the perfect complement, along with a piece of good French bread.

Ingredients

3 large heirloom tomatoes, cut into wedges

1 cup fresh blueberries

Small bunch fresh basil, rough chopped

Lemon balsamic vinaigrette

Instructions

1. Place tomatoes, blueberries and basil in a large bowl. Toss. Add to a plate and drizzle with vinaigrette.

VINAIGRETTE

Ingredients

⅛ cup aged lemon balsamic vinegar

4-6 tablespoons olive oil

1 tablespoon water

Sea salt & fresh ground black pepper, to taste

Instructions

1. Add vinegar and water to a medium bowl. Slowly whisk in olive oil. Add salt and pepper.

STEAK ON CIABATTA

WITH CARAMELIZED
ONIONS & BLEU CHEESE

Serves 4-6

Every now and then you get a craving for a hearty sandwich. And this one was created to satisfy even the biggest of appetites. The melding together of herbs and pairing it with onions and bleu cheese - you get with I mean.

Ingredients

1 ½ - 2 lbs. flank steak

Dried herb mélange consisting of oregano, basil and thyme

1 teaspoon coarse Kosher salt

4-6 cloves fresh garlic, chopped

¼ cup dry red wine

1 medium onion, chopped

1 large Spanish onion, sliced

3 tablespoons olive oil, for marinade

2-3 additional tablespoons olive oil

Mixture of 2 tablespoons brown sugar, plus ½ teaspoon cayenne pepper

4 oz. crumbled bleu cheese

Instructions

1. Using a very sharp knife, cut away the skin and excess fat from the steak. Cut tiny crosswise slits on surface of steak. Rub a teaspoon of coarse kosher salt into the slits on both sides. Place in a glass pan. Add garlic and chopped onion over top of steak. Mix together wine and 3 tablespoons of olive oil. Pour wine over steak. Cover pan with plastic wrap and place in refrigerator for at least 30 minutes.

2. Meanwhile, heat a sauce pan and add 2-3 tablespoons olive oil. Add sliced onion to pan and sauté until caramelized. Set aside.

3. Remove steak from pan and blot with a paper towel to remove excess liquid. Heat a large cast iron skillet to very hot and add a coating of olive oil. Rub herb mixture into steak. Sear on both sides. Transfer to a baking sheet. Coat with brown sugar and cayenne mixture. Place in a preheated 375-degree oven and bake until sugar mixture bubbles; about 10 minutes. Do not overcook. Remove from oven and allow to rest for 5 minutes before slicing. Slice steak against the grain.

4. Serve with caramelized onions and crumbled bleu cheese on a toasted ciabatta roll.

FARRO

WITH CURRY & APRICOTS

Serves 4-6

There are times when you have a taste for something good, but can't quite figure out what it is. Such was the day when I created this recipe. This is one of those recipes that is good as a very flavorful main dish, or as a side dish to serve with any kind of meat or fish. It is also quite tasty at room temperature.

This is a good dish to make ahead and heat up just before serving. Add a simple green salad and dinner is served.

Ingredients

1 ½ cups farro, cooked

1 medium onion, chopped

2 cloves finely chopped fresh garlic

⅔ cup chopped dried or fresh apricots

2 teaspoons good curry powder

Kosher salt and coarse ground black pepper, to taste

½ cup coconut milk

2 tablespoons olive oil

Instructions

1. Heat heavy sauté pan and add olive oil. Sauté onion until translucent. Add garlic and sauté an additional minute. Add farro. Add coconut milk and mix completely. Add salt and pepper. Cook on low heat for an additional 2 minutes, stirring constantly until heated through. Toss in apricots. A great side dish for grilled salmon or fish.

HEARTY ROASTED ROOT VEGETABLE SOUP

Serves 4-6

This is one of my favorite soups to make after the Christmas holiday season as I try to get back on track from all of the wonderful foods shared with family and friends.

It is very simple to make and yet very hearty and satisfying. And because it is one-hundred percent vegetables, it is also guilt-free.

One of the secrets to this soup is to roast off all the ingredients in a heavy Dutch oven to get that rich earthy flavor.

Ingredients

2 large bulbs fennel

2 large yellow onions

6 cloves garlic

Olive oil

Fresh or dried thyme

Sea or Kosher salt

Fresh ground black pepper

Parmesan cheese shavings or croutons (optional)

Instructions

1. Remove outer portion of fennel, cut away stalks and set aside. Cut fennel in half and then into medium chunks. Peel onion and cut into medium chunks. Peel and chop garlic cloves.
2. Drizzle olive oil into bottom of large Dutch oven; enough to coat the bottom. Add vegetables and thyme, season with salt and pepper and drizzle with additional olive oil; just enough to coat tops of vegetables. Toss to coat completely. Cover with lid.
3. Place into a preheated 375-degree oven and roast until vegetables cook completely. They will begin to brown slightly - this is the result you are looking for. Be sure to toss vegetables occasionally throughout roasting process to prevent burning.

4. Remove pot from the oven and with a hand masher, mash ½ cup of the vegetables. You can also add to a food processor if you prefer a creamy soup.
5. Add 4 cups hot water to vegetables. Simmer on low heat until the broth has a slightly creamy consistency.
6. Serve. Top with shavings of parmesan cheese or croutons if desired.

GRILLED CHICKEN ON CIABATTA

WITH APRICOT CHUTNEY & BRIE

Serves 6-8

As temps begin to drop and the summer garden is slowly winding down, there is nothing more satisfying than a nice meal to remind you of all the wonderful flavors that await you in the fall. This recipe is especially satisfying because it makes use of some of those amazing onions that should now be just right for the first digging and fresh apricots that are still in season; depending on which region of the country you live in.

This sandwich is hearty enough for dinner when accompanied with a green salad or it also works well for lunch for bigger appetites.

Ingredients

4 chicken breasts

½ cup white wine

⅛ cup olive oil

Fresh or dried herbs - basil, thyme and oregano

Kosher salt and fresh ground black pepper

6 garlic cloves, chopped

1 large yellow onion, chopped

1 tablespoon white vinegar

Instructions

1. Butterfly chicken breasts by splitting lengthwise; do not cut completely through. Place in a large zip lock plastic bag or a large bowl. Add remaining ingredients and marinate for at least ½ hour.
2. Remove marinated breasts and sear in a very hot pan until browned on one side. Place in a preheated 350-oven to finish cooking until done; about 10 minutes.
3. Remove from oven, place on a split ciabatta roll. Top with 2 Tablespoons apricot chutney (recipe follows) and a slice of brie. Place on a cookie sheet and place in oven. Allow to bake until cheese melts.

APRICOT CHUTNEY

Ingredients

12 dried prunes, cut into medium chunks

24 dried apricots, cut into medium chunks

1 small yellow onion, chopped

6 tablespoons balsamic vinegar

1 tablespoons white vinegar

½ teaspoon kosher salt

½ teaspoon fresh ground black pepper

2 tablespoons light brown sugar

5 tablespoons olive oil

Instructions

1. Heat 2 tablespoons olive oil in a large sauté pan. Add onions and sauté until tender. Add garlic and sauté for an additional minute. Add prunes and apricots and sauté until juices begin to release. Add brown sugar, vinegars, kosher salt and pepper. Stir. Cover pan and simmer for about 5 minutes.
2. Remove top and continue cooking until mixture begins to form a thick sauce. Cool and store in airtight container in refrigerator until ready to use..

RUSTIC FLATBREAD PIZZA

Serves 6-8

When we purchased our *farm in the city* we were without a kitchen for the first four months after moving in. Thankfully, it was in late spring and it was during this time that I became quite adept at what to cook on the outdoor grill. This recipe for flat bread pizza is especially good when cooked outdoors and don't be afraid to experiment with all of your favorite toppings. Be sure to use lots of good olive oil and remember, fresh is always best.

Ingredients

2 cups lukewarm water

1 tablespoon active dry yeast

1 tablespoon raw sugar

1 cup brown rice flour

2 cups all-purpose flour

1 cup whole wheat flour

1 cup oatmeal flour

1 teaspoon sea salt

3 tablespoons Olive oil

Instructions

1. Add dough attachment to stand mixer. Add warm water to bowl of a stand mixer or a large bowl if planning to mix by hand. Add yeast to water and whisk until mixed well. Add sugar to yeast mixture. Allow to rest for about 5 minutes to activate yeast. Add salt and oil. Mixture will form foam or bubbles once activated. Sift all flours together.

2. Gradually add flours to yeast mixture and combine until it forms a slightly firm dough. Knead dough for 4-5 minutes until dough becomes elastic. Turn into a large bowl that has been covered with a light coating of oil. Cover with plastic wrap or a damp cloth. Allow to rest in a warm area until doubled in size. Roll out dough on a floured surface. Place dough onto a cookie cooling rack or pan. Brush with olive oil. Add a thin layer of marinara or pizza sauce along with your favorite toppings. Bake in a 350-degree oven or on a preheated grill until done. Remove from oven, allow to rest for at least 5 minutes before cutting.

CURRY
LENTIL STEW

Serves 6-8

Winter calls for a meal that is full of flavor and satisfying for big cold weather appetites. And this recipe does not disappoint on either front. This will by far become one of your family favorites; just as it has for ours. There is usually an abundance of sweet potatoes harvested from our garden that add such a fresh and hearty richness to this dish.

Serve with cornbread slathered in butter – just a smidgeon, if you are watching calories – and you are one happy camper.

Ingredients

2 lbs. sweet potatoes, peeled and cubed

1 teaspoon olive oil

1 large onion, chopped

2 large carrots, scraped and chopped

3 cloves garlic, minced

1 teaspoon fresh ginger, minced

1 ½ tablespoon curry powder

½ teaspoon turmeric

¼ teaspoon cinnamon

3 ½ cups vegetable broth

1 ½ cups lentils

½ cup coconut milk

Instructions

1. Heat a large Dutch oven and add olive oil. Add onion and garlic and sauté until just tender. Add sweet potatoes and carrots and sauté for 2 minutes. Add spices, lentils and vegetable broth. Bring to a low boil. Lower heat. Cover with lid and simmer until potatoes and lentils are completely done. Add coconut milk, stir and heat through to finish.

AVOCADO, TOMATO, & PEACH SALAD

Serves 4-6

When it's hot outside, no one wants to get stuck in a hot kitchen or hover over a hot grill. The fresh clean taste of this recipe is just enough to satisfy cravings for something flavorful, without leaving you with a full feeling that only weigh you down. This recipe goes well with grilled shrimp or salmon.

Ingredients

1 large avocado, peeled, pitted and cut into bite-size pieces

2 large ripe yellow peaches

Ripe plum tomatoes cut into quarters

Kosher salt

Fresh ground black pepper

Balsamic Vinaigrette w/ herbs

Instructions

1. Put all ingredients in medium glass bowl. Add salt and pepper; toss. Add to serving plates and drizzle with balsamic vinaigrette. Garnish with fresh basil leaves.

BALSAMIC VINAIGRETTE

Ingredients

¾ cup extra–Virgin olive oil

¼ cup balsamic vinegar

1 teaspoon dried basil

1 teaspoon oregano

1 teaspoon thyme

1 teaspoon rosemary

1 teaspoon kosher salt

1 teaspoon fresh ground black pepper

4 tablespoons water

Instructions

1. Put all ingredients in small glass bowl. Whisk together and drizzle over salad.

HEARTY TOMATO SOUP

WITH COCONUT MILK

Serves 6-8

Coconut milk has become one of my favorite ingredients over the years when the recipe calls for cream. The subtle sweetness that is naturally found in coconut, is especially good to smooth out the acidity of tomatoes. If you want to make it extra decadent, serve with a dollop of concentrated coconut cream and spike with a dash of cayenne pepper.

Ingredients

4 cups very ripe tomatoes, chopped

½ cup sun-dried tomatoes

5 tablespoons tomato paste

1 teaspoon honey

4 cloves garlic, finely chopped

10 cloves roasted garlic, mashed

1 tablespoon cumin

1 teaspoon each, oregano, basil, thyme

1 ¾ cups coconut milk

Olive oil

Instructions

1. Heat a heavy duty pot or Dutch oven until hot. Add olive oil and onions. Sauté onions until transparent. Add garlic and sauté an additional minute. Add tomato paste and allow to brown slightly. Add dried herbs and stir. Heat through. Add tomatoes, sun dried tomatoes, roasted garlic, honey and cumin. Simmer for 5 minutes. Add coconut milk. Reduce heat and simmer on low for 15 - 20 minutes. If necessary, add a little water to reduce thickness.
2. If desired, top with croutons to serve.

AVOCADO *ON* WHOLE GRAIN BREAD

Serves 4-6

As long as it is fresh and good, I will find a way to make it a part of my southern culinary repertoire. So is the case of avocado. To tell the truth, it was not until I was in college that I ventured beyond what I was accustomed to eating at home and, in doing so, found what is now one of my favorite foods. Because I am not a meat eater, I will typically find ways to harness goodness by seeking unusual ingredients in order to create new ways to satisfy my picky palette. The good news is, my family, who are meat eaters, seem to gladly follow along.

Ingredients

6 slices whole grain bread, toasted

2 ½ ripe avocados, sliced

Fresh spinach leaves

Sun-dried tomato, pesto mayonnaise

Instructions

1. Spread pesto mayonnaise (recipe follows) on 3 slices of bread
2. Add spinach leaves and then avocado slices.
3. If desired, squeeze a little lemon juice over avocado.
4. Top with remaining slices of bread. Serve.

SUN-DRIED TOMATO BASIL PESTO MAYONNAISE

Ingredients

½ cup Dukes mayonnaise (regular or reduced calorie)

¼ cup sun-dried tomatoes, chopped in food processor

3 tablespoons basil pesto

1 tablespoon chili oil

¼ teaspoon kosher salt

Instructions

1. Combine all ingredients in a small bowl and mix together with a spoon until well-blended. Store in an air-tight container and refrigerate until ready to use.

PENNE PASTA

WITH SPICY MUSHROOM MEDLEY

Serves 6-8

This recipe is by far one of my favorites when I am in the mood for pasta.

The richness of Portobello mushrooms and the mouthwatering flavor of roasted garlic and sweet peppers will have your family begging for seconds. If you prefer not to use cream, coconut milk makes a great substitute and gives the overall flavor of the dish a tropical richness that lends itself to decadence of the savory kind.

Ingredients

1 box whole grain penne pasta

1 lb Portobello Mushrooms, sliced

4 red bell peppers, roasted

2 whole bulbs garlic, roasted

1 medium red onion, chopped

Fresh thyme

¾ cup half and half milk

¾ cup grated Parmesan cheese

½ teaspoon ground nutmeg

Olive oil

Kosher Salt and fresh ground black pepper to taste

Instructions

1. Cook pasta according to instructions on box, drain, rinse and set aside. Heat a large skillet and add two tablespoons olive oil. Add red onion and sauté until caramelized. Add mushrooms and sauté until just tender. Remove from heat.
2. Squeeze garlic from bulbs and mash into onion. Chop bell peppers and add to mixture. Add fresh thyme, approximately 1 teaspoon. Return to heat (medium). Add cheese, half and half, and nutmeg, stirring until mixture becomes slightly thickened.
3. Season with salt and pepper; to taste. Pour pasta into a large serving dish. Add vegetable mixture to pasta and toss until well-blended. Top with additional black pepper, if desired and shavings of fresh parmesan cheese. If desired, top with croutons to serve.

"Every smart southern girl knows, you can catch more bees with a touch of honey than with the tart bite of vinegar"

SWEET TOOTH

The holidays can be stressful on the wallet but it does not have to be. Growing up with a grandmother who knew how to make merry with just a little taught me how to be creative in the kitchen.

One of the things I love about Christmas is the time I get to spend in my kitchen baking and cooking up all kinds of deliciousness to share with family and friends. From my Decadent Brownies to my Thumbprint Cookies, and, of course, Pecan Bars, gifts from my kitchen makes gift giving special. Not just for my family and friends, but it brings me joy to be able to share!

Sweetie's Strawberry Shortcakes
Mary Helen's Bourbon Walnut Cake
Aunt Janie's Jam Cake
Country Apple Pie
Peach Cobbler with Lavender Cream
Lemon Lavender Tea Cookies
Grandma Lula's Sweet Potato Pie
Red Velvet Cake
Rich Southern Pound Cake
Chocolate-Chocolate Cake
Jammie Butter Nut Cookies
Pecan Bars
Southern Carrot Cake with Cream Cheese Frosting
Decadent Brownies
Blackberry Cobbler
Signature Pie Crust

SWEETIE'S STRAWBERRY SHORTCAKES

Serves 4-6

After my grandparents died, I went to live with my aunt and uncle who became my parents and it was with them that I lived until I graduated from high school and went away to college.

Eula Lonon, whom everyone called Sweetie because, you guessed it, she was a sweet soul who knew how to love up on everyone, became the woman whom I would refer to as my *mother in love*. Sweetie was not the kind of cook who explored a lot with different recipes, but the things she did make, she made extremely well. Her signature dishes were chicken and dumplings, sweet potato pie and strawberry shortcake. And although as a teenager, I was the one you could find most weekends baking cakes, pies or cookies, when Sweetie made her recipe for Strawberry Shortcake, I quickly made my exit out of the kitchen to allow her to work her incredible magic.

Her recipe for this southern favorite was more like a sweet biscuit that was then filled with fresh strawberries and covered in fresh whipped cream.

I have altered the recipe a bit by using butter as the fat for the biscuit and I also added one of my favorite flavorings, rose water, causing the strawberries to light up your taste buds when you bite into this divine dessert.

Ingredients

2 ½ cups unbleached, all-purpose flour

1 stick unsalted butter

½ cup organic cane sugar

1 ½ tablespoons baking powder

1 teaspoon salt

More Ingredients

¾ cup whole milk

3 pints fresh strawberries, hulled and quartered

½ cup organic cane sugar

1 cup heavy whipping cream, plus 1 ½ teaspoons sugar

½ teaspoon rose water

Instructions

1. Preheat oven to 425 degrees. Line a baking sheet with parchment paper.
2. Add quartered strawberries, sugar and rose water to bowl and stir to combine. Cover and set aside.
3. In a large mixing bowl, sift together flour, salt, baking soda and baking powder. Stir in sugar. Make a well in the center of flour and using a pastry blender or a fork, cut butter into flour until mixture looks likes small peas. Using a fork, add milk to mixture, stirring enough to incorporate and bind dry and wet ingredients together. Do not over work the dough. Turn dough onto a lightly floured surface and gently roll to ½ inch thickness. Using a round or square biscuit cutter, cut into small cakes and transfer onto parchment lined cookie sheet.
4. Beat an egg slightly and apply egg wash to top of cakes and bake in oven for about 15 minutes or until done. The length of time will depend on your oven so watch carefully to avoid burning.
5. Remove from oven and place on a rack to cool.
6. Add whipping cream to a mixing bowl. Add sugar and whip until cream forms soft peaks; but not too stiff. Split shortcakes crosswise. Place each shortcake onto individual serving dishes or on a serving dish. Dividing evenly, spoon strawberries on bottom half of shortcake. Add about two tablespoons of the whipped cream. Cover each with the tops of the shortcakes and drizzle some of the liquid from the strawberries over the top. Top with a dollop of whipped cream. Serve immediately.

TIP: Shortcakes can be prepared in advance and frozen for up to a week. To use, remove from freezer and allow to come to room temperature and assemble.

MARY HELEN'S BOURBON WALNUT CAKE

Serves 8-10

One of the things I love about my life is the opportunity I get to meet some of the most fascinating people. And Mary Helen was by far one of my favorites.

A classically beautiful southern belle, her smile lit up the antique shop where she spent most of her final days. I was taken aback by her spirit, although she was confined to a wheel chair and the toll that arthritis had taken on her petite body was nothing short of heartbreaking. What was so impressive about Mary Helen was once we became engaged in conversation the deformity of her body was transformed into this being that exuded all the beauty that permeated her soul. As is usually the case when I meet people, we began to talk food and by the end of the conversation she entrusted her recipe for this delectable cake with the promise that I would see to it that it lived on. And live, it will. Here's to you Mary Helen and the spiky sweetness you left us all.

Ingredients

1 ½ cups cake flour

1 ½ cups granulated organic sugar

2 sticks butter, room temperature

5 large eggs

½ cup bourbon

1 cup black walnuts, chopped

¾ cup whole milk

Instructions

1. In the bowl of a stand mixer, add butter and beat until fluffy and light. Add sugar in 3 parts, beating until light and creamy. Add eggs, one at a time, beating after each. Add flour in 3 parts, alternating with milk until well-blended. Fold in walnuts. Pour into a tube or loaf cake pan that has been oiled and floured. Bake in preheated 350-degree oven for 45 - 50 minutes or until toothpicks inserted into center comes out clean.

2. Let cake rest for 5 minutes and invert onto a cooling rack that has been placed on a large piece of aluminum foil to catch bourbon sauce.

3. To make sauce, add ½ cup of sugar and ¼ cup bourbon in a small sauce pan. Heat over low flame. Using a long skewer, prick holes throughout cake. Pour bourbon sauce over top of cake and allow to soak.

4. Using a long skewer, make holes through cake. Drizzle bourbon sauce over cake allowing the sauce to soak in. Allow cake to cool and serve.

AUNT JANIE'S JAM CAKE

Serves 6-8

This is one of my family's favorites and has all the qualities of an exceptional dessert. The flavor is simple, yet tantalizing, delicate in texture, but full-bodied, and a generous slathering of jam filling in between the layers brings on the decadence that every true dessert lover craves. To add an element of freshness, during strawberry season, a few fresh slices finishes it off just right. Not too sweet and oh so satisfying, this family dessert has stood the test of time.

Ingredients

3 cups cake flour or 3 cups all-purpose flour with 1 teaspoon corn starch

3 sticks unsalted butter, softened

2 cups raw cane sugar

4 eggs, room temperature

1 cup whole milk, room temperature

1 teaspoon baking powder

½ teaspoon baking soda

½ teaspoon sea salt

1 ½ teaspoons vanilla extract

1 teaspoon lemon extract

Grated rind of 1 lemon

1 cup apricot or strawberry preserves, plus 1 Tablespoons Curacao Orange Liqueur

Orange Liqueur Cream Cheese Frosting

Instructions

1. Cream butter in a large mixing bowl using a stand or hand mixer. Add sugar in three parts and cream for about 3 minutes after each addition until light and fluffy. Add eggs one at a time, beating thoroughly after each addition. Beat another 2 minutes.
2. Sift together flour, baking powder, baking soda and sea salt. Add extracts and lemon rind to milk and stir to combine. In three separate parts, add flour mixture and a milk to butter/sugar mixture, alternating each until combined. Beat for one minute.
3. Pour in 3-9" cake pans that have been oiled and floured and bottoms lined with parchment paper. Bake in a preheated 350-degree oven for about 25-30 minutes or until cake springs back when lightly touched or a toothpick inserted in center comes out clean.
4. Remove from oven and let rest for about 5 minutes. Invert onto a cooling rack and allow to cool completely.
5. Whip jam in a small bowl until loose and spreadable. Add jam between cake layers and frost with cream cheese orange liqueur frosting.

CREAM CHEESE ORANGE LIQUEUR FROSTING

Ingredients

2 sticks unsalted butter, softened

8 oz. cream cheese, room temperature

4 cups confectioner's sugar, sifted

1 tablespoon orange liqueur

Instructions

1. Add butter to the bowl of a large stand mixer or glass bowl (if using a hand mixer). Beat butter until smooth. Add cream cheese and beat until smooth. Add confectioner's sugar a cup at a time and mix until blended. Add orange liqueur and mix until well-blended.

COUNTRY APPLE PIE

Serves 8

Apple-picking season officially kicks off the beginning of the fall season around our house. Nothing comes close to biting into a fresh-picked apple or better yet, slicing up a few to bury on a bed of flaky crust, topped off with a nice scoop of vanilla bean ice cream. Now if that doesn't make your mouth water, surely nothing can.

Ingredients

8-10 Granny Smith apples, peeled, cored and sliced

1 cup sugar

⅔ cup corn starch

Pinch Salt, about ¼ teaspoon

1 tablespoon cinnamon

1 teaspoon nutmeg

Juice of ½ small orange and ½ lemon

½ teaspoon grated lemon rind

½ teaspoon grated orange peel

4 tablespoon unsalted butter

2 Signature Pie Crust recipes

Instructions

1. Preheat oven to 350-degrees.
2. In a large bowl, combine apples, sugar, corn starch, salt, cinnamon, nutmeg, lemon juice, orange juice and rinds. Toss until apples are completely coated. Pour into a deep-dish pie pan that has been lined with a chilled crust. Do not cut the edges off the crust to fit the pan just yet. This will happen later.
3. Dot with butter. Cover the pie mixture with the second pie crust and seal the crusts together by either crimping or fluting to secure the seal. Make small 3 inch slits across the top of the crust. Brush with an egg wash.
4. Place pie onto a baking sheet that has been lined with aluminum foil or parchment paper to catch the spills. Bake in a 350 degree oven for about 45 minutes or until the mixture begins to bubble over with caramelized juices.

PEACH COBBLER

WITH LAVENDER CREAM

Serves 6

I am a "southern peach"! That is to say, if I have to choose a peach from any place in the world, it would be a southern peach for sure. And if I could choose which state it would come from, my first choice, hands down, would be Georgia; with South Carolina peaches coming in at a distant second. Georgia peaches are meaty in texture with not a lot of water and they make the best peach pies and cobblers ever.

My grandmother was a Georgia peach, and she had peach trees that grew amazing peaches around our home. I recall however, that when family visited from Georgia during the summer they always came bearing the gift of a couple bushels of peaches for cobbler, preserves and jams.

Now, that does not mean that peaches from beautiful California, Virginia, Florida or Jersey are not good too, but if you are a peach connoisseur as I am, you will be able to tell the difference.

These days, I simply love early summer when the peaches on our peach trees ripen and I need only to make a visit outside to my Virginia garden.

This recipe for peach cobbler is a version I grew up with. I have added a couple of flavors to give it a my own farm girl kick, topping it off with fresh lavender cream using fresh lavender from the garden.

Ingredients

3 lbs. soft ripe peaches, peeled and sliced

2 cups granulated organic sugar

2 teaspoons cinnamon

1 teaspoon nutmeg

⅓ cup corn starch

More Ingredients

⅛ teaspoon fine kosher salt

Grated orange rind from 1 medium orange

2 Tablespoons orange juice

2 Tablespoons lemon juice

5 Tablespoons unsalted butter, diced

Instructions

1. Add all ingredients in a large mixing bowl. Stir until well-blended. Transfer peaches to a 9x13 baking dish. Dot top of peaches with diced butter.
2. Cover peaches with prepared pie crust that has been rolled out to cover pan completely. Flute edges of crust sealing edges as you flute. Brush top with egg wash. Cover a large cookie sheet with a piece of parchment paper or aluminum foil to catch spills. Place cobbler on top of covered cookie sheet.
3. Bake in preheated 350-degree oven for 45-50 minutes or until mixture begins to bubble over. Liquid will be thickened and crust browned when cobbler is done.

TIP For a very light and easy cobbler, top with puff pastry instead of pie crust. You can find puff pastry in most supermarkets in the frozen food section of the store.

LAVENDER CREAM

Ingredients

1 half pint fresh whipping cream

3 Tablespoons superfine organic sugar

1 teaspoon fresh lavender florets, finely chopped

½ teaspoon rose water

Instructions

1. Pour whipping cream into the bowl of a stand mixer or mixing bowl if using a hand mixer. Whip on medium speed gradually adding in sugar. Add rose water and lavender. Place in a glass or metal bowl, cover with plastic wrap and chill until ready to use. Spoon over top of each serving of peach cobbler.

LEMON LAVENDER TEA COOKIES

Serves 6-8

The warm summer months call for something light and refreshing with just a hint of tart and sweet. One of my favorite summer desserts is lemon-lavender cookies served up with a scoop of sherbet or gelato. The flavors alone will cool you down. The wonderful thing about these cookies is you can make up a double batch, freeze the extras and they are almost as good as they day you baked them.

Ingredients

2 cups unbleached all-purpose flour

1 ½ sticks unsalted butter, cut into small pieces

½ cup raw sugar

1 teaspoon crushed fresh or dried lavender

Zest from 1 lemon, finely grated

1 teaspoon fresh lemon juice

Instructions

1. Add flour and butter in a large mixing bowl and blend together using your fingers until flour and butter are combined. Add and blend sugar into flour mixture, pressing through with your fingers. Add lemon juice, zest and lavender and blend well, forming a ball. Continue to work the dough until smooth throughout.
2. Dust a cutting board or counter surface with a little flour, but not too much. Roll out dough on the surface to about ¼ inch thickness, pressing together in the areas that separate. Cut out the dough using your favorite cookie cutter. Using a spatula, transfer to a cookie sheet that has been lightly buttered or lined with parchment paper. Place in 350-degree preheated oven and bake for 8-10 minutes or until lightly browned around the edges. Remove from the oven and allow to rest for a couple of minutes on the cookie sheet. Using the spatula, transfer cookies to a cooling rack to cool.

GRANDMA LULA'S SWEET POTATO PIE

Serves 6-8

My grandmother was a huge influence on me. When I tell you that the flavors I experienced growing up made an indelible mark on my taste buds, it's an understatement. Most people who know me know that I have extremely high standards when it comes to food and that means that given a choice, I prefer that it be made from scratch. Which brings me to this - my grandmother's recipe for sweet potato pie. A great number of cooks and chefs, when making this traditional southern dessert often use sweet potato yams from the can, but when you have had the real thing, nothing compares to the richness of the flavor you get from fresh baked sweet potatoes.

Having said that, if it is more convenient for you to use canned sweet potatoes, by all means do so, but, if given the option, choose to go for the flavor!

Ingredients

3 medium sweet potatoes, baked

1 stick butter, melted

1 12-oz. can Carnation evaporated milk or half 'n half

2 teaspoons vanilla extract

2 teaspoons nutmeg

Pinch of salt

2 teaspoons lemon juice

Lemon zest, from ½ lemon

2 eggs, slightly beaten

1 cup sugar

9" unbaked pie crust

Instructions

1. Scrub and wash sweet potatoes to remove dirt under cold running water. Wrap each potato separately in aluminum foil and bake in a 350 degree oven until done. To test for doneness, give the potato a squeeze or insert a fork into the center of each potato.
2. Peel potatoes and add to the bowl of a stand mixer or if using a hand mixer add to a large mixing bowl. Add butter, eggs, sugar, nutmeg, vanilla extract, salt, lemon juice and lemon zest. Mix until well blended. Slowly add milk or half 'n half.
3. Add pie filling to pie crust. Place unbaked pie on a cookie sheet and bake in a preheated 350 degree for 45-50 minutes, or until a toothpick insert in the center of the pie comes out clean. Cool and serve.

RED VELVET CAKE

Serves 8-10

There are a number of versions of this southern classic, however, the original southern recipe calls for good cocoa to give it that undeniable rich flavor. And if you are really want to make it southern, top it off with pecans. Personally, I like it in its original form in order to savor every bite of the rich flavor.

Every year around Christmas, I can count on my sister Sheila to call with a request for the recipe although, I remind her to put it in a safe place for keeping. I will make certain she has a copy of my cookbook, thereby removing any excuse for her not having it on hand. On second thought, maybe I'll just take the call, just to experience the wonderful fellowship of talking with my sister all over again.

Ingredients

1 ½ cups sugar

2 cups vegetable oil

1 cup buttermilk

1 teaspoons white vinegar

2 tablespoons dark cocoa

1 oz. red food coloring

1 teaspoon baking soda

2 eggs, slightly beaten

2 cups all-purpose flour

1 teaspoon salt

1 tablespoon vanilla extract

Instructions

1. Combine sugar and oil in a large bowl. Add vanilla, vinegar and food coloring. Mix until combined.
2. In another bowl, sift together dry ingredients. Alternate dry ingredients with buttermilk, adding to sugar and oil mixture. Mix well. Add eggs and mix well.
3. Pour into two prepared oil and floured 9" cake pans. Bake in preheated 350-degree oven for 40-45 minutes or until cake is done. Test doneness by inserting a toothpick in the center of each cake. If toothpick comes out clean, it is done.
4. Invert cake onto a cooling rack to cool completely. Frost with cream cheese frosting.

CREAM CHEESE FROSTING

Ingredients

8 oz. cream cheese, room temperature

2 sticks unsalted butter, softened

1 teaspoon vanilla extract

4 cups confectioner's sugar (sifted)

Instructions

1. Add butter to the bowl of a stand mixer or a large mixing bowl. Blend until light and fluffy, using the paddle attachment. Add cream cheese in four portions, mixing well after each addition.
2. Reduce speed of mixer to low and add confectioner's sugar mixing until well-blended and slightly fluffy. Blend in vanilla extract to finish.

RICH SOUTHERN POUND CAKE

Serves 8-10

One of my fondest memories of dessert time while growing up is that of a slice of pound cake with fresh strawberries and whipped cream for Sunday supper. To this day, this is by far my favorite cake dessert. As the warm temperatures set in and the first strawberries begin to appear on the vine, I typically look for a reason to bake up this family mainstay.

This basic recipe has been passed throughout my family and each household has put their own spin on the original to make it their own. My cousin Yvonne passed it down to me and now I get to share it with the world.

Ingredients

1 lb. unsalted butter, room temperature

4 oz. cream cheese

3 cups organic or regular white sugar

3 cups cake flour

¾ teaspoon baking powder

½ teaspoon salt

8 large eggs, room temperature

1 teaspoon pure vanilla extract

1 teaspoon pure lemon extract

Instructions

1. Preheat oven to 325 degrees
2. Prepare Bundt cake pan by lightly oiling pan with shortening or cooking spray designed for baking. Add approximately 1 tablespoon all-purpose flour to pan and distribute flour by lighting tapping and rotating pan until completely covered. Tap pan to remove excess flour leaving only the flour coating.
3. In a large stand mixing bowl, using the paddle attachment, beat butter 1 stick at a time, until creamy. Add cream cheese in two portion, beating well after each addition. Add sugar in 3 portions, beating well after each addition. Beat until mixture is light and fluffy. Add eggs, one at a time, beating in each about 1 minute.

4. Sift together cake flour, salt and baking powder. Add flour into butter mixture in 3 portions. Beat until mixture is light and fluffy; about 5 minutes. Add vanilla and lemon extract. Beat another minute.

5. Pour cake batter into prepared cake pan. Gently rap pan on counter to remove any air bubbles. Bake in a preheated oven for 50-55 minutes or until cake is done. Test for doneness by inserting a toothpick in the center of the cake. Toothpick will come out clean when done.

6. Remove cake from oven and allow to rest on a cooling rack for 3-5 minutes. Invert cake onto rack to cool completely.

CHOCOLATE-CHOCOLATE CAKE

Serves 8-10

I confess, I am a chocolate snob! I like my chocolate dark and a cocoa content of at least 98%. There is an art to making a good chocolate cake and one of the first lessons I learned was that good chocolate will allow the cake to stand on its own. Distractions such as lots of sugar are not necessary if your ingredients are just right. This recipe is absent of flour and uses very little sugar. It is especially good when served with fresh raspberries and just a heaping spoonful of fresh whipped cream. Can't you just taste it! Ok, I digress. Here's to deliciousness!

Ingredients

14 oz. semi-sweet dark chocolate (Merken's if available)

2 oz. dark unsweetened chocolate

1 cup unsalted butter

½ cup organic sugar

9 large eggs, separated

¼ teaspoon cream of tartar

1 ½ tablespoons instant coffee or espresso

1 teaspoon pure vanilla extract

Instructions

1. Preheat oven to 300 degrees. Cover the bottom of a spring form pan with foil (you will need to remove the bottom in order to wrap) Replace bottom and snap to close. Grease bottom and sides of pan and dust with flour. Set aside.
2. Melt chocolate in a double-boiler or in a glass bowl set over a pot of simmering water. Melt butter and add to chocolate. Stir until it becomes a smooth mixture and chocolate is completely incorporated. Stir in vanilla and coffee until well-blended.
3. Add egg yolks and sugar to bowl of a stand mixer. Using the whisk attachment, beat until it becomes a very light yellow and like custard; about 8-10 minutes. Add chocolate to egg yolk mixture and incorporate completely.
4. Transfer chocolate mixture to a large bowl and completely wash and dry mixer bowl and whisk. Make sure the bowl and whisk are completely dry. Add egg whites and cream of tartar to bowl and whisk until they form soft peaks.
5. Gently fold egg whites in thirds into the chocolate mixture. Pour into prepared spring form pan. Bake 35-40 minutes. Do not overcook.
6. Transfer cake to a cooling rack to cool. Using a knife that has been dipped in hot water and dried, run along sides of cake to loosen from pan. Chill cake in cake pan in the refrigerator; preferably overnight.
7. Serve with fresh raspberries and fresh whipped cream.

JAMMIE BUTTER NUT COOKIES

(THUMBPRINT COOKIES)

Serves 8-10

This recipe is just one reason why I look forward to cooler temperatures because it gives me the perfect excuse to pull out the cookie sheets! This cookie is buttery and tender on the inside with a subtly crisp outer coating and is very simple to make with a flavor that is simply amazing!

Ingredients

1 ½ cups unsalted butter, softened

2 cups raw granulated sugar

3 eggs, room temperature

2 teaspoons pure vanilla extract

4 cups all-purpose unbleached flour

1 teaspoon baking soda

½ teaspoon salt

1 egg white plus 1 tablespoon water

¾ cup finely chopped pecans, almonds or other nuts

Raspberry or your favorite jam

Instructions

1. Preheat oven to 350-degrees. To make the cookie, in a large bowl of an electric stand mixer, beat butter on medium speed, adding sugar in slowly. Increase speed and beat until light and fluffy. Reduce speed to medium, add eggs and vanilla, beating until blended.

2. Combine flour, baking soda and salt. Add to butter mixture and mix until combined. Refrigerate until dough is completely cooled and firm; about 2 hours or overnight. Mix egg white and water in a small bowl. Spread nuts onto a plate or parchment paper.

3. Spoon dough into walnut size pieces and flatten slightly. Roll dough in egg white mixture. Roll dough into nuts to coat the dough. Place cookie onto an ungreased cookie sheet about 2 inches apart. Bake until brown around the edges, about 7-10 minutes.

4. Remove cookies from oven and with small teaspoon, indent cookie in the center. Spoon jam into the center of the cookie and return to oven. Bake an additional 3-5 minutes or until cookie is browned completely. Remove from oven and cool on a cooling rack.

PECAN BARS

Makes 24 bars

I am sure it is obvious that I love to bake — breads, cookies, cakes and pies. If it can be mixed, shaped or cut, I am one happy camper. These pecan bars are oh so good and you will want to share them again and again. And they are incredibly easy to make.

On a skill level of 1-10 with 10 being the highest, the level of skill required is about a 3. The topping is a nice chewy caramel with a thin layer of crunchiness that is sure to satisfy any sweet tooth. It also packages up nicely for your gift-giving. A single batch will yield approximately 2 dozen bars.

Base Ingredients

1 cup all-purpose flour

½ cup firmly packed brown sugar

½ cup butter

Filling Ingredients

¼ cup flour

½ cup firmly packed brown sugar

2 eggs, slightly beaten

½ cup dark corn syrup

1 teaspoon vanilla

¼ teaspoon salt

1 ¼ cups chopped pecans

Instructions

1. For the base, add all ingredients to a food processor and pulse until mixture resembles the texture of small peas. Add this mixture to an 8-inch square greased oven-proof baking pan. Bake at 350 degrees for approximately 20 minutes.

2. In the meantime, mix all ingredients together well for the filling. Pour this mixture over baked base, return to oven and bake an additional 25-30 minutes or until top is set. Cool on a wire rack. Loosen and turn onto a cutting surface. Cut into bars.

SOUTHERN CARROT CAKE

WITH CREAM CHEESE FROSTING

Serves 8-12

This carrot cake recipe has been a staple in my family for generations and was among one of the most popular desserts on the menu for my bakery. To freeze, cut into serving slices and wrap slices individually. However, chances are there will be no leftovers once you sink your teeth into this very moist and decadent dessert.

Ingredients

1 ½ cups Canola Oil

2 cups organic sugar

2 teaspoons ground cinnamon

2 teaspoons vanilla extract

1 teaspoon sea salt

2 teaspoon baking soda

½ cup flaked coconut

2 cups grated carrots

¾ cup crushed canned pineapple, in natural juice

3 eggs, beaten

2 cups sifted all-purpose flour

1 cup chopped pecans

Instructions

1. Preheat oven to 350 degrees. Lightly coat 2 10-inch cake pans with oil. Dust with flour and tap to remove excess flour from pan. Set aside.
2. To prepare cake, combine sugar and oil in a large mixing bowl. Add cinnamon, vanilla extract, and grated carrots. Sift together dry ingredients. Add to wet ingredients. Add coconut, pineapple and eggs. Stir to combine. Fold in pecans.
3. Pour into prepared cake pans and bake until done, 35-40 minutes. When done, remove from the oven and rest for 5 minutes. Remove cake from pan onto a cooling rack and allow to completely cool. Frost with cream cheese frosting (recipe follows).

CREAM CHEESE FROSTING

Ingredients

2 8-oz. packages cream cheese, room temperature

1 stick unsalted butter, softened

6 cups confectioner's sugar, sifted

1 teaspoon pure vanilla extract

Instructions

1. Add butter to a large mixing bowl. Beat until creamy. Add cream cheese in portions; beating to incorporate after each addition. Beat in confectioner's sugar, one cup at a time, making sure to blend after each addition. Once sugar has been incorporated, beat in vanilla.

DECADENT BROWNIES

Serves 10-12

There is always a good excuse to indulge in good chocolate and this brownie recipe will have you indulging every chance you get. For the best results, try making this a day ahead of time. Be sure to cool completely, wrap with plastic wrap after cooling and store in refrigerator overnight. Remove the next day and cut into squares or bites.

Ingredients

6 large eggs

2 ½ tablespoons instant coffee granules

2 tablespoons pure vanilla extract

2 ¼ cup organic sugar

15 oz. unsweetened Merkens dark chocolate, finely chopped

8 oz. semi-sweet chocolate chips

1 lb. unsalted butter

1 cup all-purpose flour

1 tablespoon baking powder

1 teaspoon sea salt

1 ½ cup chopped pecans

Instructions

1. Preheat oven to 350 degrees. Lightly oil a metal rectangular shallow baking pan measuring 13x18.
2. In a large mixing bowl, beat together eggs, coffee, vanilla and sugar. Add chocolate to a separate glass bowl. Melt butter to hot but not boiling and pour over chocolate. Let rest for a couple of minutes.
3. Stir to combine chocolate and butter. Add to egg mixture by quickly stirring in a small amount to bring temperature up to warm. Add remaining chocolate mixture to egg mixture and stir to blend completely.
4. Sift together flour, salt and baking powder. Fold flour into chocolate/egg mixture. Add pecans to a separate small bowl. Dust with a little flour to coat the nuts. Fold nuts into brownie mixture.
5. Pour into prepared pan. Bake for 30-35 minutes. Halfway through or when brownies rise, rap pan to remove air from brownies to make more dense.
6. Remove from oven and place on a cooling rack to cool completely.

BLACKBERRY COBBLER

Serves 6-8

Blackberries, in my opinion, are among the fruit of the gods. Just the thought of gathering these luscious beauties from the wild to whip up in a cobbler and top with a nice scoop of vanilla ice cream, is enough to sink me into a state of blissful delight. And, if that is not enough to make your mouth water, then consider burying a spoonful of blackberry jam between layers of hot-out-of-the-oven biscuits. But then, I digress.

This recipe for blackberry cobbler is best when made with fresh blackberries, although if fresh are not available, frozen berries are a good second best. When selecting berries, be sure to choose berries that are ripe, plump and deep in color for the maximum sweetness.

Ingredients

36 oz. fresh blackberries

1 ½ cups organic sugar

1 tablespoon ground cinnamon

¼ teaspoon salt

1 teaspoon almond extract

4 tablespoons cornstarch

6 tablespoons unsalted butter

Signature Pie Crust

Egg wash

Instructions

1. Combine first 6 ingredients in a large mixing bowl. Pour into a medium baking dish. Cut butter into small chunks and dot over the top of blackberry mixture. Roll out prepared signature pie crust and place on top of blackberry mixture. Flute the edges to seal. Brush top with egg wash using a pastry brush.

TIP To make egg wash, beat one egg and 1 teaspoon of water with a fork until well blended.

SIGNATURE PIE CRUST

Makes 1 10-inch pie crust

Every good baker knows that the secret to an amazing pie, is an amazing crust. An exceptional pie crust must be light, flaky and the right thickness to complement the filling. This pie crust recipe can be modified; depending on if your recipe is sweet or savory. For savory recipes, I add only a hint of organic sugar, and for sweet, usually about double.

Ingredients

2 1/2 cups all-purpose unbleached flour

1 stick unsalted butter (cut into chunks)

1/2 cup shortening

6-8 tablespoons ice cold water

1 teaspoon salt

1 tablespoon organic sugar

Instructions

1. Add flour, salt and organic sugar to a large mixing bowl. Whisk together to blend with a wire or plastic whisk. Using a pastry blender, blend in butter and shortening into the flour until mixture resembles peas. Be sure to leave some small chunks of butter to create a flaky crust. Using a fork, lightly blend in water making sure not to over mix. Using one hand, gently bind mixture to form a ball. Add dough ball to a piece of plastic wrap and wrap completely. Flatten dough to mimic a disk. Add dough to a ziplock bag and chill in refrigerator for at least an hour or overnight.
2. To use, roll out pie crust on a lightly-floured surface (butcher block or granite counter top). Using board scraper (you can find these at baking shops or online), gently lift dough from surface and place in pie shell. Flute edges or use a fork to crimp around the border. For a very flaky pie crust, place crust in the freezer until firm before baking or adding filling.

*"The coolness of ice filled glasses gently
brushing across hot brows is a gentle reminder
of the power of being refreshed"*

SIPS OF
THE SOUTH

Nothing tops off a good meal like the perfect drink. It should be full of flavor, not too sweet, and a complement to whatever you are dishing up.

These are just a few of the favorite drinks around our house. Bear in mind too that you can make these healthier by making a spritzer; using carbonated water in 3 parts and 1 part drink. Not only is it very refreshing on a hot day, but it is also healthier, in the long run.

Sweet Tea
Floral Lemonade
Frozen Strawberry Lemonade
Mint Julep
Sparkling Cranberry Punch
Lavender Sugar

SWEET TEA

Serves 6-8

I have to admit that I tend to like my drinks with just a hint of sweetness, however, when it comes to tea, most southerners will tell you, the sweeter the tea the better.

The secret to a good sweet tea is a very strong steeped tea and a good simple syrup. This recipe can be the base for all kinds of additions, with raspberries being a favorite among sweet tea lovers.

Serve over ice with lots of lemon on the side.

Ingredients

10 tea bags, Tetley or Lipton

1 cup water

2 cups sugar

2 cups water

Lemon slices

Instructions

1. Add 1 cup water to a small pot and bring to a boil. Turn off flame under pot and add tea bags. Allow to steep for at least ten minutes or more. Meanwhile, in another pot, add 2 cups water and 2 cups sugar and bring to a simmer. Stir to combine sugar and water. Allow to simmer for about 5 minutes. Turn off flame and allow to sit until cooled.

2. Add tea and simple syrup to a large pitcher. Add additional water to fill. Stir. Refrigerate until completely chilled. Serve over ice cubes with sliced lemon.

TIP Be sure to only drink this periodically since the high sugar content makes this not the healthiest to consume on a regular basis. Instead, save for those special get-togethers and opt instead for my lemonade or raspberry lemonades which can be cut with sparkling water to reduce the sugar.

FLORAL LEMONADE

Serves 6-8

Sweet tea and lemonade are traditional beverages of the South and this recipe has an amazing ingredient that I discovered in my travels many years ago. Rose water gives whatever you add it to a floral note that will take your taste buds on a trip to paradise.

Ingredients

1 cup sugar

1 cup water

1 teaspoon Rose Water

½ cup lemon juice

Peel from 2 lemons, remove pith or white part from peel

Instructions

1. Remove outer skin from two of the lemons and carefully remove the white portion of peel. Soften lemons by rolling on counter top. Squeeze lemons and set aside juice. In a small pot, add sugar, water and peel from lemon. Place pot on stove over medium heat. Bring to a slow boil and reduce to simmer. Cook for about 10 minutes to form a syrup. Cool.
2. Pour lemon juice, rose water and syrup mixture into a large pitcher. Fill pitcher with water. Stir. Serve over crushed ice in tall glasses. Top each glass with fresh mint leaves and thin slices of lemon.

TIP To make a fizzy lemonade, mix 3 parts sparkling water to 1 part lemonade in each glass. Rose water can be purchased at most Middle Eastern specialty stores or online.

FROZEN STRAWBERRY LEMONADE

Serves 6-8

On a hot day, nothing refreshes like something sweet and tart to lower the temperature. This recipe for strawberry lemonade is a favorite around our house and I am almost certain it will become a favorite around your house too.

Ingredients

8-10 large strawberries, stems removed and quartered

1 cup Simple Syrup

1 ½ cups fresh squeezed lemon juice

1 teaspoon Rose Water

6-8 cups water

Ice Cubes

Instructions

1. Add strawberries, syrup, lemon juice and rose water to a blender and blend until completely pureed. Add to this 6 cups water and ice cubes. Blend until ice cubes are completely crushed and mixture is consistency of a loose slush. Serve with fresh mint leaves.

MINT JULEP

Serves 4-6

In the mood for a good southern libation? You are going to love this classic recipe for Mint Julep. And remember, you only need a little to make a good impression.

Ingredients

10-12 mint leaves

2 teaspoons superfine sugar

Seltzer Water

Crushed Ice

2 oz. Bourbon Whiskey

Instructions

1. Add leaves to the bottom of an old-fashioned glass and add sugar. Using a spoon crush the leaves and sugar together to make a nice mixture. Add a splash of seltzer. Fill glass with crushed ice and bourbon. Add additional seltzer. Garnish with fresh mint leaves.

SPARKLING CRANBERRY PUNCH

Serves 10-12

The sweet, tart flavor of this punch along with the vibrant color makes this refreshing drink a real hit. To add an extra note of flavor, add a cinnamon stick and cloves to the syrup while steeping.

Ingredients

1 cup sugar

1 cup water

½ cup fresh cranberries

½ cup fresh orange juice

32 oz. sparkling water

Instructions

1. To make syrup, add sugar and water to a small pot and bring to a low boil. Add cranberries. Simmer for 3-5 minutes. Remove from heat and allow to rest for 10 minutes. Strain cranberries and retain liquid. This will become your base/syrup for the punch. For a larger serving, simply double the ingredients.
2. Add cranberry syrup, orange juice and sparkling water to a large punch bowl. Serve.

LAVENDER SUGAR

Makes 1 Cup

Warm summer months render the fragrant lavender florets, that are the star ingredient for this wonderfully fragrant sugar. Keep on hand to sweeten your favorite hot or cold tea, or if you are feeling adventurous, use to add a high flavor note to icy lemonade.

Ingredients

1 cup organic sugar

2 tablespoons fresh lavender florets

lavender sprigs

Instructions

1. Add sugar and lavender florets to a small mixing bowl. Combine. Transfer sugar to a ½ pint canning jar. Top with lavender sprigs. Seal. Place on shelf until ready to use. Use to sweeten tea or for baking sugar cookies.

KITCHEN NOTES

From cutting boards to stand mixers, if you are going to cook, you have to have the right tools. Having said that, the kind of equipment you will need is totally dependent on how much time you plan to spend in the kitchen. With the help of my Professional Chef's Guide (Culinary Institute of America), I have compiled an inventory of tools that might help to make your time in the kitchen most enjoyable. Keep in mind too that it is not necessary to purchase this entire list of equipment, but rather use it as a guide of what you might want to consider.

Knives

Tips
1. Handle knives carefully.
2. Sharpen your knives often.
3. Keep your knives clean.
4. Use surfaces designed for cutting avoiding cutting on metal, glass or marble.

Knife Types

Chef's or French Knife
Utility Knife
Paring Knife
Boning Knife
Filleting Knife
Slicer
Cleaver
Tourne Knife

Hand Tools

Rotary or Swivel-Bladed Peeler
Kitchen Fork
Whips/Whisks
Offset Spatula
Pastry Bag

Small Equipment

Graduated Measuring Pitchers
Weight Scale
Thermometers
Measuring Spoons

Miscellaneous

Colander
Mixing Bowls
Storage Containers

Rolling Pin
Manual Meat Tenderizer
Cookie Cutters
Turkey Baster
Kitchen Shears
Cooking Spatulas and Spoons
Ladles
Skimmers
Cork Screw
Tongs
Large Palette Knife
Scoops
Zester
Vegetable Scraper
Swivel Peeler
Cookie Cutters

Pots and Pans

Types of Materials
Copper Pots
Cast Iron Skillet
Stainless Steel
Aluminum

Types
Stockpot
Sauce Pan
Sauce Pot

Rondeau
Omelet Pan/Crepe
Bain-Marie (Double Boiler)
Steamer

Oven Cooking Pans
Roasting Pan
Sheet Pan
Gratin Dishes
Cake Pans
Springform Pans
Loose-Bottom Tart Pans
Pie Pans
Muffin Tins
Loaf Pans
Tube Pans

Equipment

Immersion Blender
Food Processor
Food Chopper
Mandoline
Standing Mixer
Blender

INDEX

ACKNOWLEDGMENTS

Writing this book has been a labor of love. I never imagined the countless hours, days and nights that it would take in order to bring this vision to life. No good work is ever done alone. It takes the love and support of people who believe in your dreams with a willingness to faithfully travel the journey with you. I have been encouraged and supported in ways that a simple thank you seems too little. I do hope you know how much you are appreciated.

There have been so many who have stood beside me, no matter what; the following being just a few.

For your support when I contemplated giving up, many thanks to Karen Schachter, Evelyn Lugo, Donna Jones, Diane Stevens, Deborah Davidson, Thomasina Shealey, Amanda Jones, Maimah Karmo, Carlos Austin, Tanya Dallas Lewis, Tommy Whites and Alma Cash. You stepped up when it mattered!

And to my children, Darryl and Allie, you are indeed what every parent hopes for in children. You have been my cheerleaders and support throughout every chapter of this journey. You have loved and supported me, always showing up when I needed you most. Thank you for allowing me to be your mom and for being a true reflection of God's love.

To Monica and Adam, thank you for sharing your beautiful boys with us and for being a part of our family. Monica, if I had been blessed to have another daughter, I would want her to be a mirror image of you.

And to my lifelong friend, Harriet, you are my sister from another mother who has always been faithful, loving and kind. You are a true blessing in my life and I hope you know just how much you are loved.

To my sister Sheila, thank you for the countless hours spent on the phone during the difficult moments to remind me of God's love and to encourage me to share my gifts with the world.

To Sandra Martin, thank you for your light and support that has never wavered.

Thanks to April Payne, who has since I met you, consistently been a compass, to remind me to stay the course and to never lose sight of why I came here.

To Barbara Jacksier, thank you for sharing your resources and for these words spoken to me, "I want you to succeed!" I don't know if you know how empowering this was to me. You have been a huge supporter of my efforts since the day I met you and I want you to know how much you are appreciated.

To Jessica Grounds whose life is a reminder to me that the values instilled in us by our elders are indeed still very much in vogue. Thank you for your support and for your friendship.

To Tracy Johnson Murphy, for your faith in me and my vision, I will be eternally grateful.

To Kate, Rachel, and Morgan of Mascot Books, who were patient with me throughout this arduous process of turning my vision into a reality, many thanks.

And finally, to the countless others who have encouraged me along the way; you know who you are, thanks!

To the creator and maker of all good things, God, thank you!

PHOTO CREDITS &
FOOD STYLING

COVER STYLING

Soull Ogun

FOOD STYLING

Allison McDaniel

Bonnie McDaniel

PHOTOGRAPHER

Beverli Alford

SUPPLEMENTAL PHOTOGRAPHY

Sonia Malfa

Adam Jones

Cameron Whitman

Seth Blaustein

"Because life should be good.
How good is that..."

ABOUT THE AUTHOR

BONNIE MCDANIEL

Bonnie McDaniel, "Farm Girl In the City" is an accomplished chef, gardener and TV host. Her restaurant, Christina's at The Bailiwick, was a Wine Spectator Award winner, recognized for having one of the best food and wine menus in the world. Her inn, The Baliwick was also a distinguished member of Select Registry a club of the top inns in the country.

A connoisseur of all things good, Bonnie McDaniel developed her brand, "Good Living" writing about what she loves; sharing personal and anecdotal experiences on food, gardening, travel and spiritual sustenance. Having been raised by her grandparents whose livelihood was cooking and farming, she shares a food and gardening tradition rich with southern history that is relevant to contemporary well-being.

She is an author of three books, In the Eye of the Storm: A Celebration of Family and The Real Purpose of Home, Queen Bee and her newest cookbook, Farm Girl in the City – Of Food and Love (Spring 2018 release), the first in a 5 cookbook series. She is a contributing writer for Small Room Decorating, food and gardening writer for patch.com, a former editor for Family Digest Magazine and the creator and Editor-in-Chief for Recipes for Good Living Magazine.

Bonnie is an on-air food and gardening segment contributor for ABC's Good Morning Washington, Fox 5 Morning News, CBS and CNN/HLN. She has also appeared on the TODAY Show sharing seasonal recipes and best practices for the home and garden.